Baobabs

OF THE WORLD

Andry Petignat
& Louise Jasper

Baobabs

OF THE WORLD

Illustrated by Louise Jasper

To Paul,
With very Best wishes!

Andry Petignat

First published in French in Madagascar in 2012 by Arboretum d'Antsokay, B.P. 489, Toliara, 601, Madagascar and Carambole Editions Madagascar SARL, BP 5168 Antananarivo 101 Madagascar
www.antsokayarboretum.org and carambol@moov.mg
This edition published by Struik Nature (an imprint of Penguin Random House South Africa (Pty) Ltd)
Reg. No. 1953/000441/07
The Estuaries No. 4, Oxbow Crescent, Century Avenue, Century City, 7441
PO Box 1144, Cape Town, 8000 South Africa

Visit **www.randomstruik.co.za** and join the Struik Nature Club
for updates, news, events and special offers.

10 9 8 7 6 5 4 3 2 1

Publisher: Pippa Parker
Managing editor: Helen de Villiers
Editor: Emily Bowles
In-house design: Janice Evans
Translator: Louise Jasper
Proofreader and indexer: Emsie du Plessis

Reproduction by Hirt & Carter Cape (Pty) Ltd
Printed and bound by C & C Offset Printing Co., Ltd, Shenzhen, China

Print: 978 1 77584 370 2

ePub: 978 1 77584 472 3

ePDF: 978 1 77584 473 0

Front cover These *Adansonia grandidieri* bear the scars of intense bark-harvesting. They represent excellent examples of the baobab's remarkable ability to heal. Near Befandriana Sud. (A.P.)
Front cover flap The sun sets beyond the famous Avenue of Baobabs, western Madagascar. (L.J.)
Back cover At 1,600 years, this is the oldest known baobab in Madagascar. Wrinkled and stunted by countless droughts, this age-old tree has been lovingly nicknamed the 'Grandmother'. Tsimanampesotse National Park, southwestern Madagascar. (L.J.)
Page 1 A sketch of *A. suarezensis* by Louise Jasper.
Page 2 A fire blazes in the distance beyond a stand of *A. grandidieri* near the Avenue of Baobabs at night. (L.J.)
Page 3 An old postage stamp from Madagascar showing a view of the Avenue of Baobabs.
Page 5 An immense African Baobab (*A. digitata*), with an elephant for scale. Tanzania. (F.R.)
Pages 6–7 Golden-barked *A. rubrostipa* baobabs grow on small limestone tsingy islands in Moramba Bay, near Anjajavy Lodge and Reserve. (L.J.)
Page 8 Looking up to the sky between two specimens of *A. za*. Ifotaka, Mandrare Valley. (L.J.)
Pages 12–13 An old stand of *A. za* in a vast sisal plantation in the Mandrare Valley at sunset, near Ifotaka. (L.J.)

'I pointed out to the little prince that baobabs were not little bushes, but, on the contrary, trees as big as castles; and that even if he took a whole herd of elephants away with him, the herd would not eat up one single baobab.'

Antoine de Saint-Exupéry, 1943, *The Little Prince*

CONTENTS

PREFACE

The enormous baobab is one of the most iconic trees of the African continent. What few people realize is that Africa is home to just one widespread species, while the island of Madagascar possesses six wonderfully diverse species that exhibit an array of astonishing growth forms. Although Madagascar's baobabs outshine their single African cousin in terms of their variety, floral beauty and adaptability (if not in overall size), surprisingly little research has focused on their biology and commercial potential. The African species, however, has been intensively studied in recent decades. Much remains to be discovered about these huge, stem-succulent trees, but for several species threatened by human activities, time is running out.

This guide provides a brief introduction to the known species of baobab, with emphasis on the Malagasy species but also including those from Africa and Australia. The existence of a putative ninth species, *Adansonia kilima*, has been reported from Africa, but this has not been independently verified so we have decided not to include it in this book. We hope that baobab lovers will enjoy this guide, and that it will not only aid in identifying the eight species, but also play a small part in bringing these magnificent and culturally significant trees to a wider audience.

The first section of this guide begins with a short introduction to the classification and general description of baobabs, followed by details of their life history, biogeography, dispersal and role in people's lives. The second section comprises a guide to each of the eight baobab species, including a botanical description, details of their habitat, distribution and principal uses, based on information sourced from scientific literature or directly from the Malagasy people (in the case of Madagascar's baobabs) who use baobabs in their daily lives. The 120 photographs and 32 line drawings show the leaves, flowers, fruits and typical growth habit of each species. We have provided a glossary to aid understanding of some of the scientific terms used in this guide.

Baobabs of the World is not just a guide, it is a celebration of these unique, charismatic trees. We hope this book will inspire you to learn more about baobabs, or even take a special journey to visit them.

ANDRY PETIGNAT AND LOUISE JASPER
Antsokay Arboretum, Madagascar

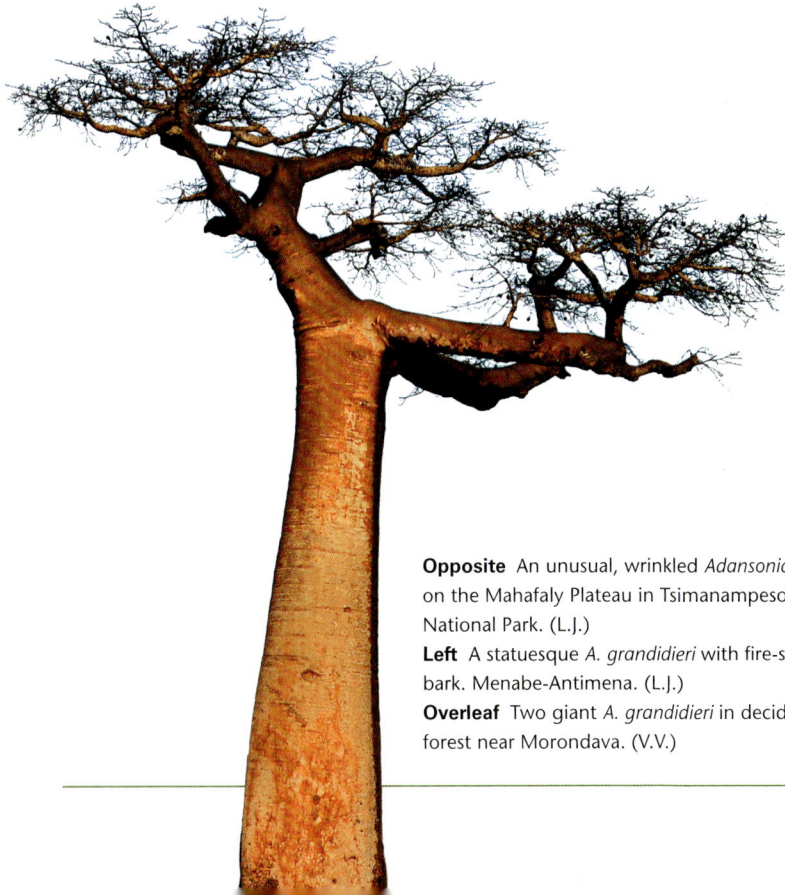

Opposite An unusual, wrinkled *Adansonia rubrostipa* on the Mahafaly Plateau in Tsimanampesotse National Park. (L.J.)
Left A statuesque *A. grandidieri* with fire-scorched bark. Menabe-Antimena. (L.J.)
Overleaf Two giant *A. grandidieri* in deciduous dry forest near Morondava. (V.V.)

ACKNOWLEDGMENTS

The production of *Baobabs of the World* would not have been possible without the generous support of the following individuals and organizations:

- The San Diego Cactus and Succulent Society, sdcss.net
- Kelly Griffin
- Anonymous donor
- Stéphane Philizot, PhileoL, info@phileol.com

Many friends and colleagues helped to improve the accuracy of this work, but we take responsibility for any errors or inaccuracies that remain. In particular we would like to thank the following people for their invaluable contributions: David Baum, Alain Bonard, Goulam Eugène, Charlie Gardner, Brian Kemble, Michel Laplace, Diana Mayne, Domoina Rakotomalala, Pierre-Jules Rakotomalaza, Antoine Rougier, Sarah Venter, Sébastien Wohlhauser.

We also thank the following people for generously contributing their photographs: Daniel Austin, David Baum, Berkeley Fitzhardinge, Charlie Gardner, Tom Gardner, Amanda Mullard, Steven Nowakowski, Christophe Quénel, Ferdinand Reus, Benjamin de Ridder, Sarah Venter, Vincent Verra and Xavier Vincke.

Finally, we would like to give special thanks to our families for their support while we put together our tribute to the magnificent baobabs.

Introduction to baobabs

DISTRIBUTION

Madagascar drifted away from Africa around 160 million years ago, during the breakup of the prehistoric supercontinent Gondwanaland. Since about 90 million years ago, the island has remained separate from other landmasses, allowing its flora and fauna to evolve and differentiate in near isolation. Madagascar has therefore inherited an incredibly rich and divergent biodiversity, with thousands of species that are found nowhere else on Earth. Of its 11,031 native plant species, 82% are endemic to the island, along with 100% of its non-flying mammals, 99% of frogs, 92% of reptiles, 65% of freshwater fishes and 52% of birds. At higher taxonomic levels Madagascar's endemism is even more impressive; with 24 endemic families of plant and animal (not including invertebrates), the island constitutes of one the world's 12 centres of megadiversity. Its biodiversity plays a fundamental role in the country's economic development and human well-being, but sadly its natural ecosystems are characterized by an extreme fragility, and habitat degradation is taking place at an increasingly alarming rate.

Baobabs illustrate the spectacular diversity, endemism and vulnerability of the Malagasy flora. Madagascar is the centre of baobab diversity: of the world's eight species, six are unique to the island (*Adansonia grandidieri*, *A. madagascariensis*, *A. perrieri*, *A. rubrostipa*, *A. suarezensis* and *A. za*). Three of these species are considered to be Endangered by the IUCN, and a further two are Near Threatened, due to extensive habitat loss, indicating the urgent need for conservation action. In contrast, the African Baobab (*A. digitata*) is found throughout the semi-arid regions of sub-Saharan Africa and has been widely planted in tropical countries around the world, including Haiti, Venezuela, India, Java and Madagascar. The eighth species, the Boab (*A. gregorii*), grows in the drylands of northwestern Australia.

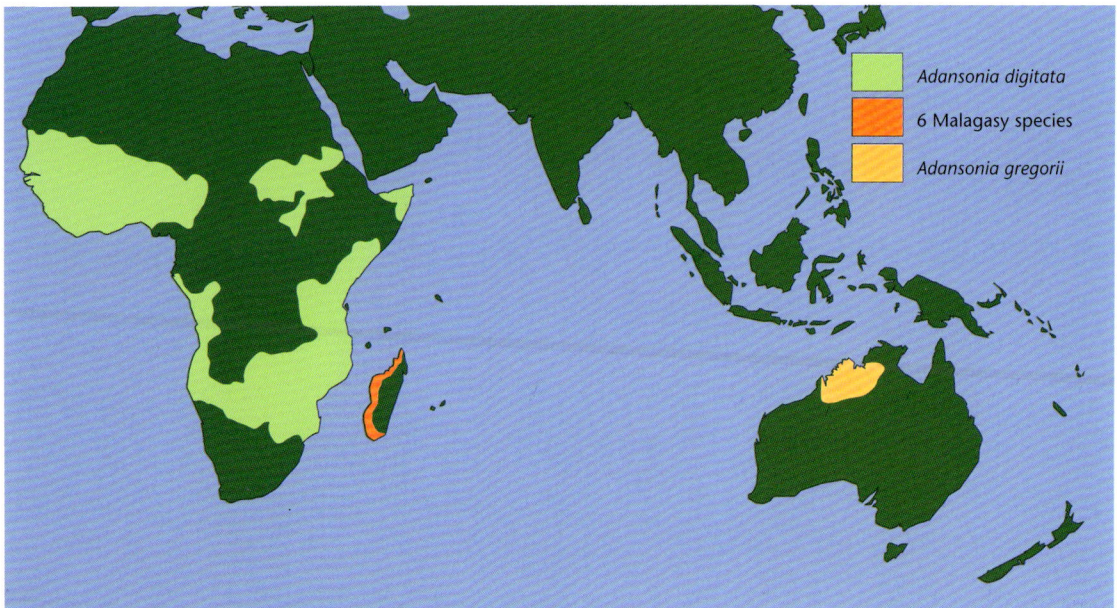

Legend:
- Adansonia digitata
- 6 Malagasy species
- Adansonia gregorii

Top left Like many other mammal-pollinated flowers, *A. grandidieri* blooms are shaped like a shaving brush. (L.J.)

Above The natural distribution of all eight species of *Adansonia*, clearly showing how much more widespread the African Baobab (*A. digitata*) is compared with the other seven species.

Previous spread Local people have carved footholds into these stunted baobabs (*A. grandidieri*) to help them gather the nutritious fruit and leaves. Andavadoaka. (L.J.)

BOTANICAL CLASSIFICATION

Baobabs (genus *Adansonia*) were formerly placed within the family Bombacaceae. However, molecular studies revealed that they should be reassigned to the subfamily Bombacoideae within the huge cosmopolitan mallow family, Malvaceae. The Bombacoideae contains 27 genera and about 250 species, the majority of which occur in the New World tropics. These include some economically important species such as the South American Balsa (*Ochroma pyramidale*), which yields one of the world's softest commercially traded hardwoods (used in model-making, aircraft and film props), and the Kapok (*Ceiba pentandra*), whose long fruits produce cotton-like fibres used as stuffing material.

Carolus Linnaeus (1707–1778) named the genus *Adansonia* in honour of the French botanist and explorer Michel Adanson (1727–1806), following the suggestion of Bernard de Jussieu (1699–1777). Although the fruit of the African Baobab (*A. digitata*) had long been known to European botanists, Adanson was the first to formally describe the tree, which he referred to as the 'calabash tree', in 1757. He based his description on information gathered during an exploratory voyage to Senegal while working for the French East India Company. He also collected a prodigious amount of information on the plants, animals, commerce and languages of Senegal.

Although the common name for trees of the genus *Adansonia* is baobab, this word is not actually derived from any African or Malagasy dialect. This name first appeared in 1592, spelled bahobab, in *De Plantis Aegypti Liber*, a book of Egyptian flora by the Italian doctor and botanist Prosper Alpino (1553–1617). In this volume, Alpino described fruits of *A. digitata* that were sold on the markets of Cairo under the name bahobab, which was likely derived from the Arabic *bu hibab* meaning 'many-seeded fruit'. When Adanson described the tree, he named it baobab in light of Alpino's work, but later this name came to be used to refer to all species of *Adansonia*.

Theodore de Bry (1528–1598) published the first record of a Malagasy baobab species in 1605 in *Indiae Orientalis*. His illustrated plates depicted peculiar, bottle-shaped trees, thought to correspond to *A. rubrostipa*, but it wasn't until the end of the 19th century that Henri Baillon (1827–1895) confirmed the presence of the genus *Adansonia* in Madagascar. In 1952, the French botanist Henri Perrier de la Bâthie (1873–1958) published the first full description of the known baobab species of Madagascar (this paper excluded *A. perrieri* which was only described in 1960 after De la Bâthie's death). Today, the seminal paper on the systematics of *Adansonia* remains David Baum's revision published in 1995.

Top The flower of the African Baobab (*Adansonia digitata*). (L.J.)

Above The fruit of the African Baobab, which is known as *bu hibab* in Arabic, giving rise to the common name baobab. (S.V.)

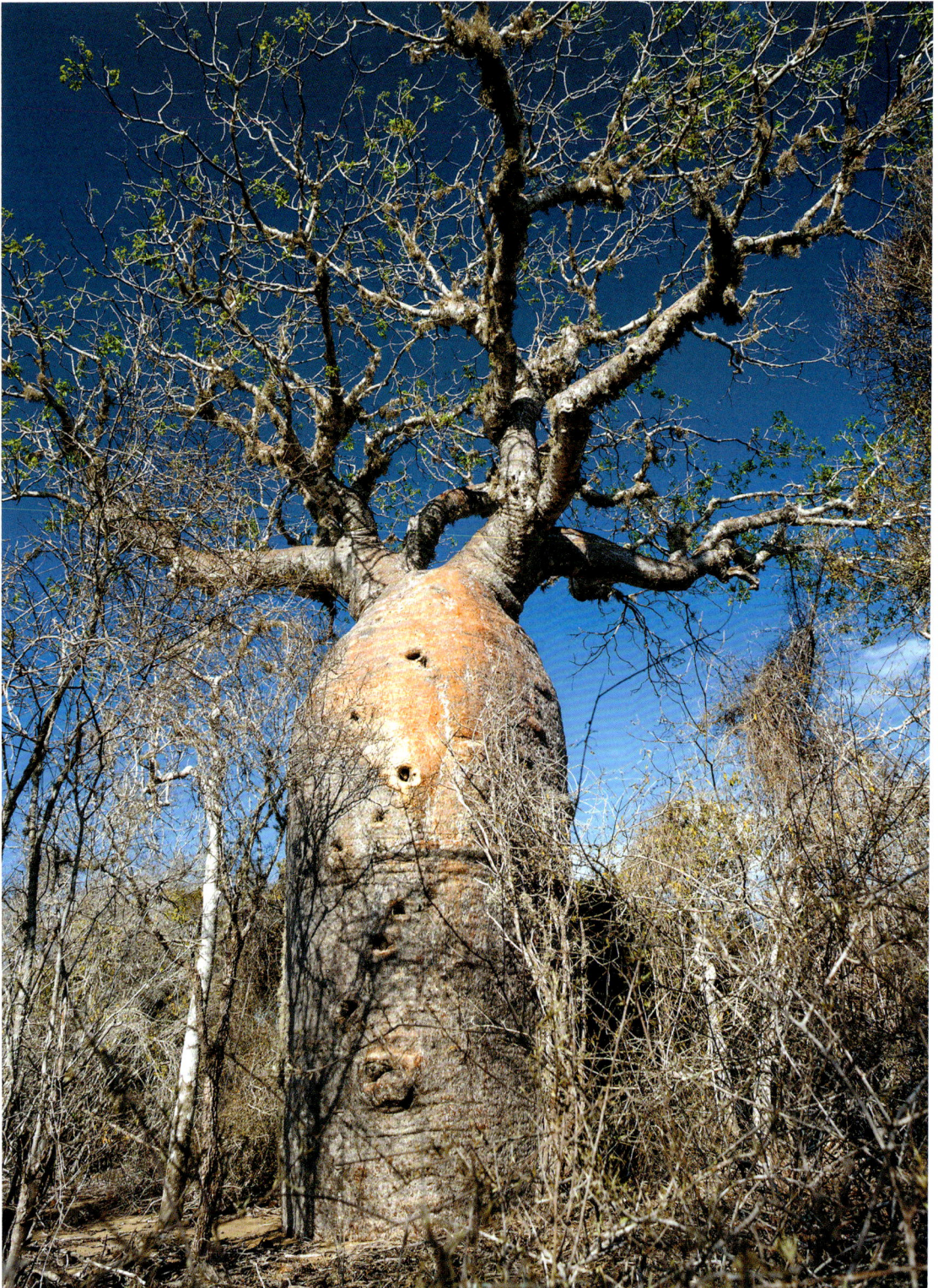

DESCRIPTION

The eight species in the genus *Adansonia* are tropical, deciduous trees with mesic, palmate leaves and perfect (hermaphroditic) flowers. They have massive, swollen trunks reaching heights of 5–30m, which tend to narrow abruptly just beneath the canopy of branches, giving the tree a bottle-shaped appearance. The trees are usually 'emergents', exceeding the height of the surrounding forest or thicket. Juvenile baobabs tend to have slender, tapering trunks that are swollen at the base. The soft, spongy wood may contain up to 79% water, while the wood of more 'typical' trees, such as the sycamore (*Acer pseudoplatanus*), may contain just 27% water.

Opposite A bottle-shaped *Adansonia rubrostipa* putting out new leaves in preparation for the rainy season. Mikea Forest. (L.J.)
Right This young *A. grandidieri* is branched and conical, typical for a juvenile baobab. (A.P.)
Below Other stem-succulents, such as *Pachypodium geayi*, are often confused with baobabs. (L.J.)

Among the largest stem-succulent plants in the world, baobabs, with their strange growth form, represent one of the most impressive adaptations to a semi-arid environment. Although it was long assumed that baobabs store water in their trunks for use during drought, recent research indicates they actually store this water for structural stability. If a baobab were to use too much water during the dry season, it might collapse under the weight of its branches! In fact, the tree seems to use a very small amount of water to produce new leaves at the end of the dry season, though these will remain inactive (i.e. their stomata stay closed) until the first rain falls. This strategy enables the tree to begin photosynthesizing immediately, taking full advantage of the short and unpredictable rainy season. Leaves are important organs, converting sunlight and carbon dioxide into vital nutrients for the plant, but they also lose plenty of water via transpiration. Therefore, baobabs drop their leaves shortly after the last rains, thus conserving water.

These spectacular trees are renowned for their twisted, root-like branches, which give them the appearance of having been planted upside down. Their actual root system is equally impressive, extending some 50m from the trunk. However, as in many succulent plants, the root systems of mature baobabs are relatively shallow, often running along the surface of the soil and rarely descending more than 2m deep. This allows the tree to take advantage of even the lightest rainfall, essential for survival in a dry climate.

Baobabs grow in numerous different habitats, but local variations in rainfall and soil quality can drastically affect their growth rate and appearance. Under more favourable conditions, for example those that prevail in the forests near Morondava, *Adansonia grandidieri* achieves the massive, columnar growth form for which it is famous, becoming up to 30m tall. On the dry, rocky limestone soils and salt pans around Andavadoaka, however, this species is reduced to

Opposite and below Dwarf specimens of *Adansonia grandidieri* in subdesert habitat near Andavadoaka. Local people harvest the nutritious leaves for cattle fodder, giving the branches a stunted appearance. (A.P. and L.J.)
Right An example of the tall, columnar growth form of *A. grandidieri* common in the Menabe region. (L.J.)

a stout, stumpy tree of just 4–5m in height. In extremely dry regions, such as the Mahafaly Plateau in southwestern Madagascar, some dwarf baobabs have developed highly wrinkled bark following years of repeated shrinkage and swelling of the trunk. Some specimens of *A. rubrostipa* and *A. grandidieri* have highly decorative bark, with intricate swirls and spirals in many shades of red, brown and yellow. These natural patterns are likely caused by fungal growth, though the phenomenon has yet to be studied.

The flowers are large, showy and fragrant, opening just before or after dusk. The ripe buds open remarkably quickly, usually within 30 minutes. In fact, the flowers of several species (including *A. rubrostipa*) can open fully in just 30 seconds – the movements of the unfurling petals are easily detected with the naked eye. Although the flowers may remain on the tree for several days, they are reproductively viable for 15 hours at the very most. The eight species in genus *Adansonia* can be divided into three groups according to the structure of their flowers: Brevitubae, Longitubae and Adansonia. Each group attracts specific types of animal pollinators that have adapted to feed on flowers in different ways.

Opposite The Grandmother Baobab is an ancient, stunted and wrinkled *Adansonia rubrostipa* from Tsimanampesotse National Park. (L.J.)

Above The flowers of the Brevitubae group (such as this *A. grandidieri* flower) are adapted to attract small mammal pollinators such as fruit bats and nocturnal lemurs. (A.P.)

Below *A. rubrostipa* flowers (like those of other species in the Longitubae group) are mainly pollinated by hawkmoths. (L.J.)

The Brevitubae group contains two species, *A. grandidieri* and *A. suarezensis*, whose flower buds are held aloft on short, erect stems. Their flowers are white and resemble a shaving brush, and are primarily pollinated by mammals such as the Madagascar Straw-coloured Fruit Bat (*Eidolon dupreanum*) and the Pale Fork-marked Lemur (*Phaner pallescens*). The Longitubae group comprises the other four Malagasy species (*A. madagascariensis*, *A. perrieri*, *A. rubrostipa* and *A. za*) and the Australian Boab (*A. gregorii*). These have long, cylindrical flower buds on erect or horizontal stems with red, yellow, orange or white petals, and are mainly pollinated by long-tongued hawkmoths. In Madagascar, the hawkmoth species *Coelonia solanii* and *Xanthopan morgani* are important pollinators of Longitubae baobabs, though the Pale Fork-marked Lemur and Fat-tailed Dwarf Lemur (*Cheirogaleus medius*) are also thought to play a role. Souimanga Sunbirds (*Nectarinia souimanga*), Ring-tailed Lemurs (*Lemur catta*) and various butterflies also visit the flowers to feed on nectar and pollen, but their manner of feeding makes them unlikely pollinators. The Boab is mainly pollinated by the hawkmoth *Agrius convolvuli*. The Adansonia group contains just one species, the African Baobab (*A. digitata*), whose pendulous white flowers are suspended on a long stalk and are mainly pollinated by fruit bats (such as *Rousettus aegyptiacus*) and, to a lesser extent, bushbabies (*Galago* spp.).

Baobabs produce quite large, round to oblong, indehiscent fruits covered with soft brown or grey hairs that feel velvety to the touch. The hard outer shell (pericarp) encloses numerous kidney-shaped seeds, which are embedded in a matrix of fibres and spongy or chalky pulp. The African Baobab is also known as the Cream of Tartar Tree, as its fruit pulp contains high levels of tartaric acid, which is used in baking. Fruit shape and size vary considerably between the different baobab species, and are also highly variable within *A. digitata*, *A. gregorii* and *A. za*. For example, *A. za* usually has oval-oblong fruits, but in some parts of its range the fruits are narrow and pointed (see first image, second row on p.100).

In Africa and Australia, baobab seeds are mainly dispersed by animals, but in Madagascar (where there is no known native animal disperser) they are likely spread via water.

Top The velvety, hard-shelled fruit of *Adansonia rubrostipa*. (A.P.)

Right A Souimanga Sunbird (*Nectarinia souimanga*) drinks nectar from an *A. grandidieri* flower. Its habit of feeding at the side of the flower means it is very unlikely to transfer pollen to the stigma, which is raised above the stamens. (L.J.)

Opposite A Ring-tailed Lemur (*Lemur catta*) consumes an *A. rubrostipa* flower. (L.J.)

Overleaf Branches of a mature *A. rubrostipa*, heavily laden with ripening fruit. (A.P.)

LIFE AND DEATH

Baobabs can grow to an enormous size, and many look incredibly ancient – but how old are they really? During his visit to the Madeleine Islands off the coast of Senegal in 1749, Michel Adanson came across two giant baobabs whose bark sported inscriptions carved by sailors in the 15th century. He estimated their annual growth rate by comparing them with younger baobabs of a known age, and concluded that these huge trees must be more than 5,000 years old. Adanson's calculations sparked lively controversy among the scientific community, including the notable explorer and missionary David Livingstone (1813–1873). The latter argued that no tree could have survived the biblical flood, which is said to have taken place just 3,500 years ago, and refused to believe that the giant baobabs could be as old as the Egyptian pyramids.

Those contentious trees no longer exist, but modern-day researchers continue to investigate the

Top and insert Baobab wood is composed of concentric sheets of fibre. Once dead, the wood decomposes rapidly. (A.P. and L.J.)

Opposite The African Baobab (*Adansonia digitata*) is the longest living angiosperm tree in the world. Kruger National Park. (L.J.)

Overleaf The sacred Andombiry Baobab (*A. grandidieri*) is the largest baobab (and possibly one of the oldest) in Madagascar with a 27.4m circumference (6m diameter). (L.J.)

age of other gargantuan baobabs. Growth-rate measurements indicate that the largest living specimens must be many hundreds of years old, but for several reasons baobabs remain very difficult to age accurately using traditional methods. Firstly, while the age of most trees can be ascertained by cutting a transverse section through the trunk and counting the annual growth rings, this method cannot be used for baobabs because of the structure of their wood, which is soft and fibrous with poorly defined growth rings. These

rings do not necessarily correspond to a yearly growth pattern; for example, older trees eventually stop laying down new rings, while the central rings may fuse or even rot away if the tree becomes hollow in old age. Also, when a baobab dies it rapidly collapses into an unsightly, fibrous heap and decomposes completely within a few years, making it difficult for researchers to study very old specimens.

Secondly, inaccuracies arise when aging a baobab based on the circumference of its trunk. The relationship between age and circumference is not necessarily linear, as the rate of growth is not constant throughout a baobab's life, and the largest trees may not be the oldest. Growth rate is also greatly affected by local environmental conditions: if we were to plant two baobab seeds of the same species in two different regions, one receiving plentiful rain and the other suffering frequent droughts, the former would grow faster and larger than the latter. In 100 years' time, the two trees would likely differ greatly in girth and height despite being the same age.

Although traditional methods cannot be used to gauge a baobab's age accurately, the advent of modern chemistry and radiocarbon dating has enabled researchers to begin to resolve the debate. For example, the famous Glencoe Baobab – a large and very old African Baobab growing in Limpopo Province, South Africa – suffered a major split in 2009, providing a unique opportunity for scientists to study its age. The researchers collected and analysed several samples from the damaged trunk, and the results were startling: the oldest samples were around 1,835 years old, making the Glencoe Baobab the oldest known angiosperm tree! Similar research was carried out on the living Grandmother Baobab in southern Madagascar, which was found to be around 1,600 years old. This research indicates that many large baobab trees may indeed be extremely old, but perhaps not as ancient as many people once believed them to be.

Opposite In the foreground lie the dry, fibrous remains of a dead *Adansonia grandidieri*. Andavadoaka. (L.J.)

Above The largest African Baobabs were once believed to be as much as 5,000 years old, but recent research suggests 1,000–2,000 years may be a more realistic estimate. (L.J.)

BIOGEOGRAPHY

The genus *Adansonia* has a disjointed distribution that baffled botanists for nearly two centuries. It is native to Madagascar, sub-Saharan Africa and Australia – landmasses that have been separated by hundreds of miles of open ocean for millions of years. Given that Madagascar is the centre of diversity for the genus, it has generally been considered to be the place where baobabs first evolved. However, if this is true, then how did baobabs arrive in Africa and Australia?

Initially, baobabs were thought to be relics of an ancient flora that had evolved more than 120 million years ago while Africa, Madagascar and Australia were connected to the Gondwanan supercontinent. When the great continent split apart, baobabs were supposedly carried around the globe on separate landmasses, giving rise to their strange distribution. However, recent studies using morphological analysis and molecular techniques have shown that baobabs evolved much more recently – some 35–90 million years ago – and must therefore have spread across the oceans after the breakup of Gondwanaland. It is now believed that the pioneering ancestors of modern baobabs sailed away from Africa as seeds, safely stowed away in their buoyant, hard-shelled fruits; one washed up in Madagascar and the other in Western Australia, where they produced new colonies that later diverged into discrete species.

The theory of long-distance oceanic dispersal is plausible given that the hard fruits of several baobab species are, at least partly, dispersed by water. Indeed, in 2006 several *Adansonia madagascariensis* trees (whose fruits float exceptionally well) were discovered growing along the southern coast of Mayotte in the Comoro Islands, just 200km from Madagascar. This finding was particularly interesting as this species is mainly found in northwestern Madagascar, the region directly facing Mayotte, so the presence of the Comorian population of baobabs is very likely the result of a successful transoceanic crossing.

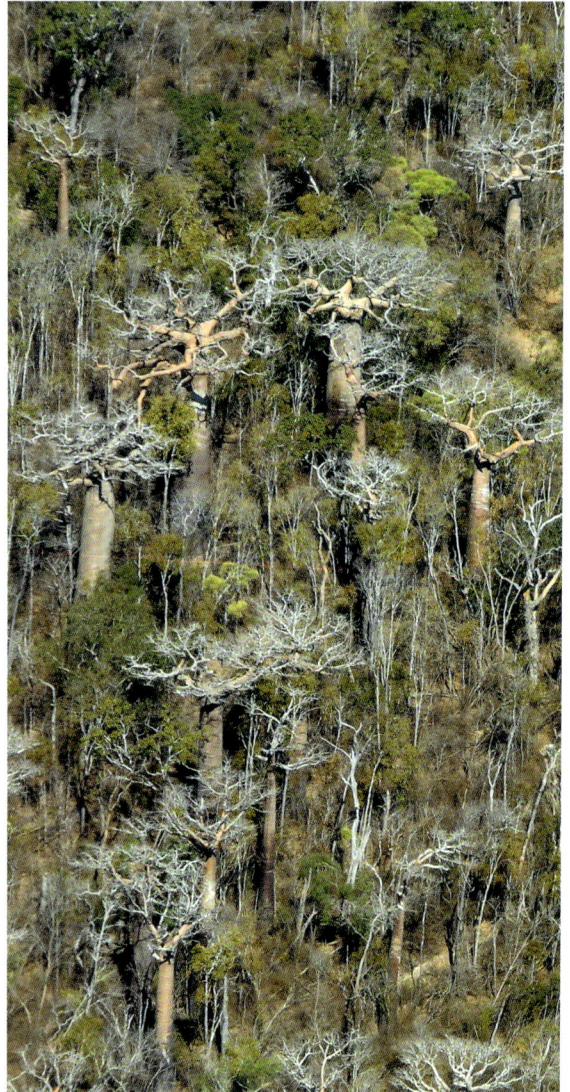

Above The 'baobab forests' of western Madagascar are dominated by three baobab species, including *Adansonia grandidieri*. Kirindy-Mite National Park. (X.V.)

Opposite Golden-trunked *A. rubrostipa* growing on limestone islands in northern Madagascar. It may have been coastal trees like these that long ago dropped their fruits into the ocean, which were then swept off to start new baobab colonies on distant shores. Moramba Bay. (C.G.)

In Madagascar, the genus *Adansonia* is distributed throughout the dry to sub-arid forests and thickets of western and southern Madagascar, from Taolagnaro in the south to Antsiranana in the north. Certain areas are particularly rich in baobabs, giving rise to their nickname 'baobab forests'. However, they are completely absent from the central highlands and the humid east coast.

Above Several baobab species, including *Adansonia grandidieri* (pictured), *A. perrieri* and *A. za*, are often found growing along watercourses and even along coastlines and mangrove forests. The fruit of these species are at least partially dispersed by water. (C.Q.)

DISPERSAL

Nowadays, young baobab trees are scarce in Madagascar's dry forests and thickets. Researchers are still trying to understand exactly why the regeneration process appears to have faltered, but it seems likely that a combination of fire, habitat degradation, grazing by cattle and goats, competition with invasive species and the excessive collection of fruits and seeds by people could be having a severe impact on baobab reproduction.

If Madagascar's baobabs are no longer effectively regenerating, it may also be that an important element in their reproductive cycle has disappeared. Their seeds, like those of many other tropical trees, are thought to be adapted to dispersal by animals – a process known as zoochory. The animal intermediary consumes the seeds whole, which then pass through its digestive tract unharmed before being expelled in the animal's faeces at some distance from the parent tree. Indeed, the African Baobab is also known as the Monkey-bread Tree, because the fruits are consumed by baboons, though other mammals such as elephants also eat and disperse the seeds. Kangaroos and wallabies are known to eat the fruits of the Australian Boab, but there are no records of Malagasy baobab fruit being consumed by any native animals. The introduced Bushpig

(*Potamochoerus larvatus*) likely consumes baobab fruit, but its method of eating almost certainly destroys the seeds. Today, Madagascar's baobabs are mainly spread via water dispersal, though human activities may also have a role. People collect the fruits for both local consumption and for sale in urban markets around the country, as they are used to make a tangy, nutritious juice. Domestic cattle (the humped zebu, *Bos indicus*), may also consume the seeds as they forage along forest paths. However, just a few hundred years ago, the island's baobabs may have been dispersed by some very different creatures.

It is possible that the baobabs' key animal disperser(s) disappeared during the wave of faunal extinctions that began around 2,000 years ago after humans colonized Madagascar. The island lost at least 34 species of large vertebrate, including 17 giant lemurs (nine genera in the suborder Strepsirhini), three pygmy hippos (*Hippopotamus*), two giant tortoises (*Aldabrachelys*) and eight elephant birds (Aepyornithidae). Likely candidates for the baobab disperser include large-bodied extinct lemurs in the genera *Archaeolemur* and *Pachylemur*, which occurred in southern and western dry forests until the arrival of humans, and survived until at least 1,000 years ago. Studies indicate these species were principally frugivorous.

Other possible candidates are the two extinct giant tortoises in the genus *Aldabrachelys*, which once occurred in large numbers in Madagascar's dry forests. The closely related Aldabran Giant Tortoise (*A. gigantea*) has been shown to readily consume baobab seeds without destroying them. The seeds then show enhanced germination once they have passed through the reptile's gut. If, as it seems, the island's baobabs do require animals for dispersal, the long-term future of these magnificent trees may be in jeopardy.

The seeds of Malagasy and African baobab species are able to withstand extreme dehydration, tolerating around 5% humidity. It is relatively easy to sow baobab seeds, but germination can be very slow due to the hard seed coat (tegument), which is largely impermeable to water, air and light. There are several methods by which one can break the dormancy imposed by the seed coat and speed up germination. One method is to cover the seeds with simmering water and leave them to soak for 24 hours before planting them. Alternatively, one can scarify the seeds by rubbing them with sandpaper, or by soaking them in undiluted sulphuric acid for several hours. The seeds of *Adansonia madagascariensis* appear to require rather more severe scarification compared with the other species.

For normal, healthy development, seedlings must be planted out in a sunny position in well-drained soil and kept moist without over-watering.

Above The different stages of germination of an *Adansonia grandidieri* seed. (L.J.)

Above right A two-year old *A. grandidieri* sapling, with a distinct water-storage tuber. (L.J.)

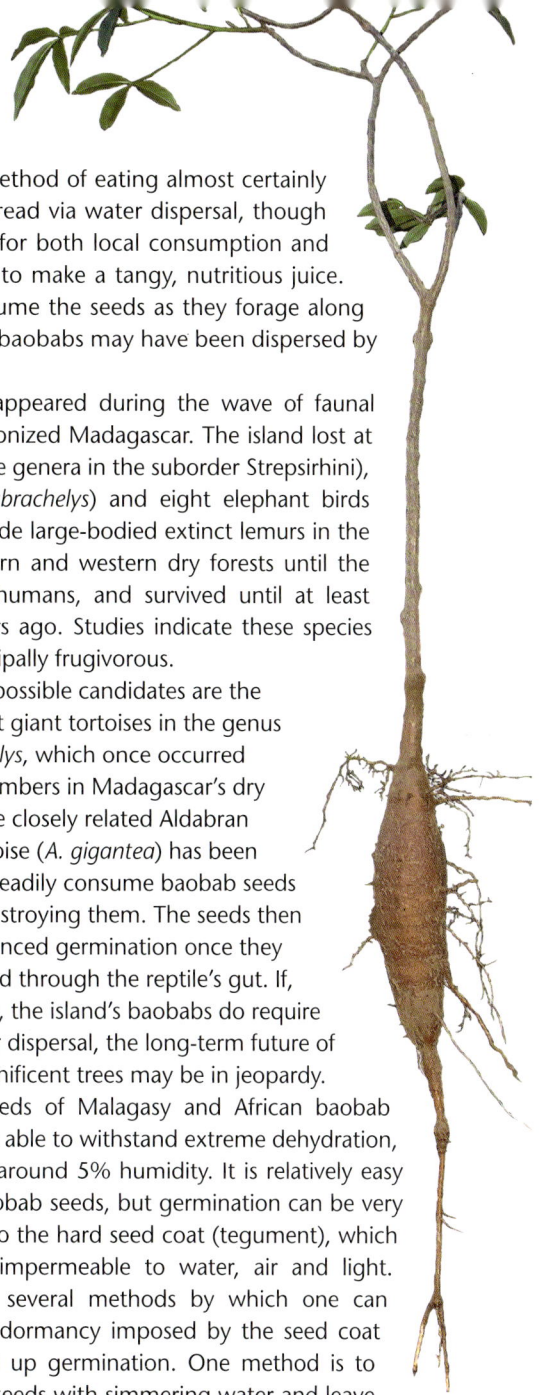

CONSERVATION

Madagascar's unique biodiversity, like that of many other floral and faunal communities around the world, is increasingly threatened by the destruction and degradation of natural habitat. Over the course of the last century, the rate of habitat destruction on the island has intensified in the wake of a population explosion. The majority of the country's 22 million people live in rural communities dependent to a large extent on natural resources for their subsistence. Traditional agricultural methods involve shifting agriculture (known as *tavy* or *hatsake* in Malagasy), in which areas of forest are cut and then burned to create new fields. These are mainly planted with rice, maize or cassava, and may be productive for two or three years. However, the loss of forest cover results in rapid erosion and leaching of the soils by rain and wind, particularly on slopes, and the fields quickly lose their fertility. After a short space of time, the cleared lands are reduced to a dry, sterile lunar landscape unsuitable for growing food crops, so the farmers must move on to another patch of forest to begin the cycle once again.

More than ever before, Madagascar's biodiversity is in need of protection. Fortunately, the government began to recognize the value of the island's natural ecosystems early in the 20th century, and the conservation movement was initiated in 1927 with the creation of 10 *Reserves Naturelles Integrales* (RNI) or Strict Nature Reserves. These RNI were established with the intention of protecting the island's major forest ecosystems, with access granted solely for scientific purposes. Later, several RNI were converted to national parks, along with a number of new sites, in order to protect a greater variety of ecosystems and sites of great natural beauty, while allowing for the development of ecotourism within the parks.

Opposite A solitary *Adansonia grandidieri* stands above flooded rice paddies, where once lay dense, deciduous dry forest. Morondava region. (V.V.)

Above The silver-grey trunks of these *A. za* stand in stark contrast with the red tilled earth, relics of the dry spiny forest that once covered this landscape. The tree on the right contains a man-made well, accessed by the ladder lying at its base. Toliara region. (V.V.)

Overleaf These *A. za* were once surrounded by subhumid forest, but this was cleared to make way for agricultural fields. The remains of this rare forest type are now protected within Zombitse-Vohibasia National Park, which is sadly still threatened by fire and shifting agriculture. (L.J.)

Conservation activities gathered momentum during the 1990s, as the preservation of biodiversity became a top priority for the Malagasy government, but it was during the World Parks Congress in Durban, which took place in September 2003, that things really took off. The participating countries underlined the importance of the contribution of protected areas to sustainable development, environmental services and to poverty alleviation, and it was in this spirit that the Malagasy government committed to tripling the size of the island's protected area network, from 1.7 million hectares in 2003 to 6 million hectares by 2012, amounting to at least 12% of Madagascar's land cover.

Across the Madagascar National Parks (MNP) protected area network, there are now 47 sites, covering 2.75 million hectares, as well as the numerous new protected areas (NPAs) that are currently being created within the framework of the Durban Vision. At the time of writing, more than 30 NPAs have been created, covering 3.34 million hectares, and a further 32 are in the planning stages, which may cover 971,000 hectares.

The dry and spiny habitats of the southern and western regions are less well represented in Madagascar's protected area network than those of the east. In 2003, only 2.3% of remaining southern spiny forest habitat was formally protected, compared with 13.3% of eastern humid forest. However, with the implementation of the Durban Vision, the proportion of dry habitats under formal protection has begun to rise. Apart from the Avenue of Baobabs near Morondava, which is now an NPA within

Above Vast expanses of baobab-dominated dry forest are cleared every year by the destructive practice of shifting agriculture (*hatsake*). (L.J.)

the Menabe Antimena Protected Landscape, there are no other sites dedicated solely to the conservation of baobabs. Nevertheless, the presence of these magnificent trees is often a key element in justifying the establishment of new protected areas, such as Kirindy-Mite National Park, whose forests boast the greatest concentration of baobabs in Madagascar, including the spectacular and Endangered *Adansonia grandidieri*.

The species *A. grandidieri*, *A. rubrostipa* and *A. za* are all well represented in Andranomena Special Reserve and Kirindy Private Reserve (both of which fall within the Menabe Antimena Protected Landscape), Kirindy-Mite and Mikea national parks, and the Mangoky-Ihotry Complex.

Adansonia za is a widespread species found in many other protected areas, including those in the west mentioned above as well as Berenty Private Reserve, Andohahela National Park and Nord-Ifotaka Protected Area in the southeast, Zombitse-Vohibasia and Tsimanampesotse national parks and Ranobe-PK32 Protected Area in the southwest.

Adansonia rubrostipa also occurs in Namoroka National Park, Ranobe-PK32 Protected Area, and in the sub-arid climate of Tsimanampesotse National Park, where stunted and often wrinkled specimens are characteristic of the spiny thicket. Towards the northern edge of its range, this species is found alongside *A. madagascariensis* in Anjajavy Private Reserve.

Adansonia madagascariensis and *A. perrieri* are both found within the Ankarana and Montagne d'Ambre national parks, Montagne des Français Protected Area and Analamerana Special Reserve. The latter two sites are also home to *A. suarezensis*, while the dry forests of Loky-Manambato Protected Landscape contain *A. perrieri*. These reserves are all of particular importance for baobab conservation, because they contain two of the rarest and most threatened species in the genus. Even though *A. perrieri* is likely more widespread than once believed, only one of the few sites at which it is found (Ambondromifehy) contains more than a handful of individuals, and only in Montagne d'Ambre are the baobabs sheltered from fires and deforestation. However, the long-term survival of the Montagne d'Ambre population is threatened by introduced rats, which eat the seeds and prevent regeneration. Only the fruits that fall in the river have a chance of being carried away from the rats and may succeed in germinating elsewhere.

Until recently, *Adansonia suarezensis* was included in just one reserve, but fortunately it is now represented within several new protected areas. However, even though it is not quite as scarce as was once thought, and despite its inclusion in the protected area network, it is still rare, with a highly restricted range, and its habitat continues to be degraded and fragmented. In addition, a recent study has predicted that climate change will have serious impacts on populations of both *A. suarezensis* and *A. perrieri* in coming decades, which, coupled with the other threats to their survival, may push them to the brink of extinction in our lifetimes.

A multiple-trunked *Adansonia rubrostipa* in spiny forest on the Mahafaly Plateau in Tsimanampesotse National Park. (L.J.)

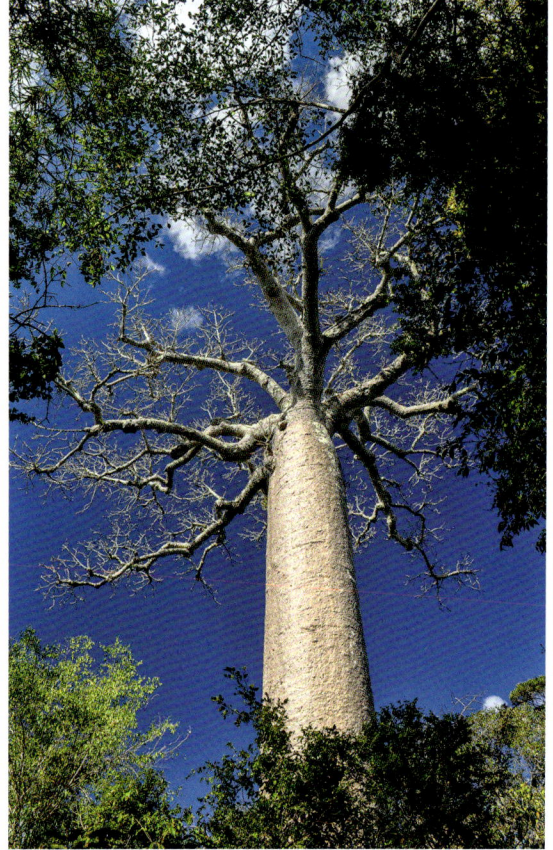

Despite national efforts to establish protected areas and conserve the island's precious fauna and flora, the main forces driving biodiversity loss persist. Not only are certain species and habitats still not represented within conservation programmes, but many protected areas also continue to be threatened by fire, logging, grazing, and shifting agriculture. One way to protect the Endangered baobabs and the island's endemic flora from extinction is to preserve their seeds in seed banks, but it is essential to conserve their natural habitat if at all possible to enable future reintroductions.

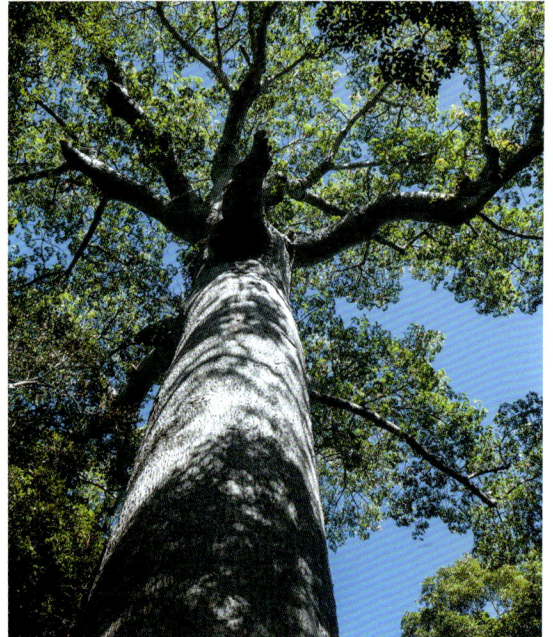

Top left and above *Adansonia suarezensis* in the Montagne des Français Protected Area and on Cap Diego. (L.J.)
Top right A statuesque *A. za* in the subhumid forest of Zombitse-Vohibasia National Park. (L.J.)
Right *A. madagascariensis* in Ankarana National Park. (L.J.)
Opposite The Avenue of Baobabs is a world famous tourist attraction containing stunning *A. grandidieri* in Menabe Antimena Protected Landscape. (A.M.)

USES

Madagascar's baobabs are much less well utilized than the African species, which is exploited locally for its leaves, bark and roots, and commercially for its fruit. This is not because the Malagasy species are less useful; in fact, they have largely the same properties as the African and Australian species, but traditionally people have harvested only their fruit, seeds and bark.

The seeds of several *Adansonia* species are rich in oil. According to Henri Perrier de la Bâthie, *A. grandidieri* seeds were exported to Marseille from 1874 until the early 20th century, where they were mixed with other oily seeds for the extraction of cooking oil. However, the supply of seeds was apparently insufficient to satisfy the market, and so the trade ceased. Villagers in the Morondava region have also been known to extract the high-quality oil from the seeds for local use. However, the oil contains fatty acids that are harmful if consumed in large quantities, which must therefore be removed or neutralized before use.

The dry fruit pulp is rich in calcium, potassium, vitamin C and tartaric acid, and can be eaten or made into a tangy, refreshing juice when mixed with water and sugar. The dried pulp of the African Baobab has recently gained popularity as a 'superfood' among health food enthusiasts in Europe and the United States, where it is added to smoothies and cereal bars to give a nutritious boost.

The bark of a mature baobab tree can reach a thickness of up to 15cm, and is composed of tough, longitudinal fibres, which are often used to manufacture rope (known as *hafotse* in Malagasy) particularly for use on zebu-drawn carts and on the traditional outrigger canoes. The spongy, water-rich wood is composed of concentric sheets of fibre and cannot be used as fuel or for construction. This is a great advantage for the trees, which are usually left standing, even in largely deforested areas. However, in times of drought,

Above A Sakalava house with a roof made with sheets of baobab wood. Near Morondava. (T.G.)
Opposite This *A. grandidieri* bears the scars of repeated bark harvesting. Near Befandriana Sud. (A.P.)

whole trees are sometimes felled so that the watery wood can be fed to cattle. Sheets of wood are harvested from dead or living trees and then dried and sold on local markets for use as thatch. Fortunately, baobabs are fantastically resilient, and though many trees show the scars from bark and wood harvesting, most recover rapidly and regrow their bark. Edible mushrooms (*Volvariella volvacea*) may be found growing at the foot of old or dead baobab trunks. Sadly, some baobabs near Toliara have been deliberately felled for the cultivation of this mushroom.

The baobabs' remarkable ability to survive severe wounds and regenerate bark is put to use in several ways. In Madagascar's arid south, people carve deep holes into baobab trunks in order to create water reservoirs or wells. These collect rain water during the rainy season for use during droughts, without which locals might perish. Local people also hammer a succession of stakes into the trunks of fruiting baobabs in order to climb up to the canopy to harvest the ripe fruits before they fall and spoil. Once the stakes rot away, the tree is left with rows of footholds. Large trees, especially *Adansonia digitata*, *A. gregorii* and *A. grandidieri*, may become hollow as they age. Such baobabs have been used in many different ways, including as storage barns, storm shelters, bars, toilets and even prisons.

Top Juice made with baobab fruit pulp is tart, refreshing, and rich in calcium and vitamin C. (L.J.)
Middle Wooden stakes hammered into a baobab's trunk enable people to climb to the branches and harvest the ripe fruit. (A.P.)
Above left and background A thin sheet of dried baobab wood, showing its loose, fibrous structure. (L.J.)
Above right Edible mushrooms (*Volvariella volvacea*) growing on a dead *Adansonia madagascariensis* tree. Ankarafantsika. (L.J.)

Left The entrance to a man-made well in an *Adansonia za*. Between Betioky and Beheloka. (A.P.)
Above The interior of the same well. (A.P.)
Bottom left The open fruit of *A. madagascariensis*, said to be the least palatable of all baobab fruit. (A.P.)
Bottom right A woman selling *A. grandidieri* fruit on the market in Toliara. (L.J.)
Overleaf African Baobab (*A. digitata*) at the centre of a roundabout in Mahajanga, Madagascar. (L.J.)

BAOBABS IN CULTURE

In light of their outlandish appearance, it is not surprising that baobabs are the subject of folklore and superstition. Numerous legends explain the baobabs' extraordinary shape. For example, an Arab story blames the devil for the tree's upside-down appearance, suggesting that long ago he pulled up the tree, planted its branches in the earth and left its roots up in the air. A legend of the San people of the Kalahari tells of the time when the Great Spirit was presenting each of the first peoples and animals with a different type of tree to plant. Arriving late, the hyena received the only tree that was left, the baobab. The hyena was so furious that he planted it upside down. A widespread African legend tells us that when God planted the baobab, it continued to wander around the countryside. One day, God became annoyed and decided to plant it upside down to keep it firmly rooted in one place. Another legend describes how the baobab arrived in dry habitats: God planted the baobab next to a pool, but it complained continuously about being too wet. God became so irritated with the complaints of the ungrateful tree that he pulled it out and threw it down into the dry regions of the land.

In contrast with native African peoples, Australian aborigines do not really have a concept of God, and their legends and beliefs about baobabs tend to relate to specific trees rather than the species in general. Certain Boabs are linked to stories of the ancestor creators; some are believed to embody dark powers and are used in spells, while others sport drawings and carvings of important spirits and ancestors from the Dreamtime.

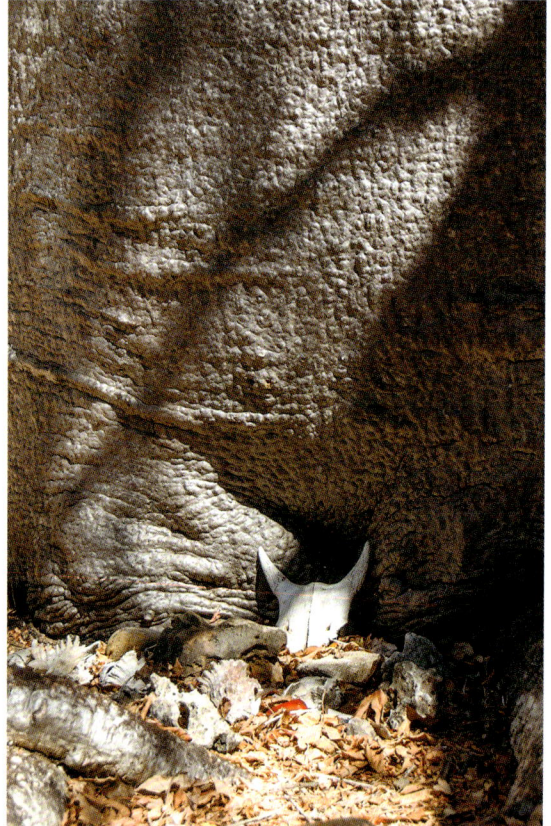

Above Offerings laid at the base of the great sacred African Baobab (*Adansonia digitata*) on a small island in Moramba Bay. Sadly, this tree collapsed in 2014. (C.G.)
Opposite An old *A. grandidieri* on the edge of a seasonal pool near Andranomena Special Reserve. It is considered sacred by the local Sakalava people. (L.J.)

Certain baobabs in the forests of southwestern Madagascar are considered to be inhabited by the sacred spirits of the ancestors, or by forest spirits such as the *kokolampo*. The latter may possess passers-by, particularly elderly people, who wander too close to the tree. Giant African Land Snail (*Achatina fulica*) shells may be arranged at the base of sacred *A. grandidieri* trees to indicate their special status and receive offerings of rum. Other offerings are placed at the tree in return for blessings, such as food to ensure a good harvest, money for good fortune and rum for fertility and general prayers. Some baobabs with suggestive protuberances, such as the sacred tree at Lake Andranovorinampela in Andranomena Special Reserve, are visited by couples wishing to have a baby. The forests surrounding these sacred giants are protected by the local people, who ensure that the powerful ancestor spirits are respected.

Today, the iconic image of the baobab appears in many areas of modern life in Africa, Madagascar and Australia, including company logos, administrative emblems, postage stamps, banknotes and in marketing and commercial products. Mainland Africa in particular has an ever-increasing trade in all things baobab, including cosmetics and food supplements. The trees have also been the source of inspiration for numerous artists and writers, and are the subject of many traditional proverbs.

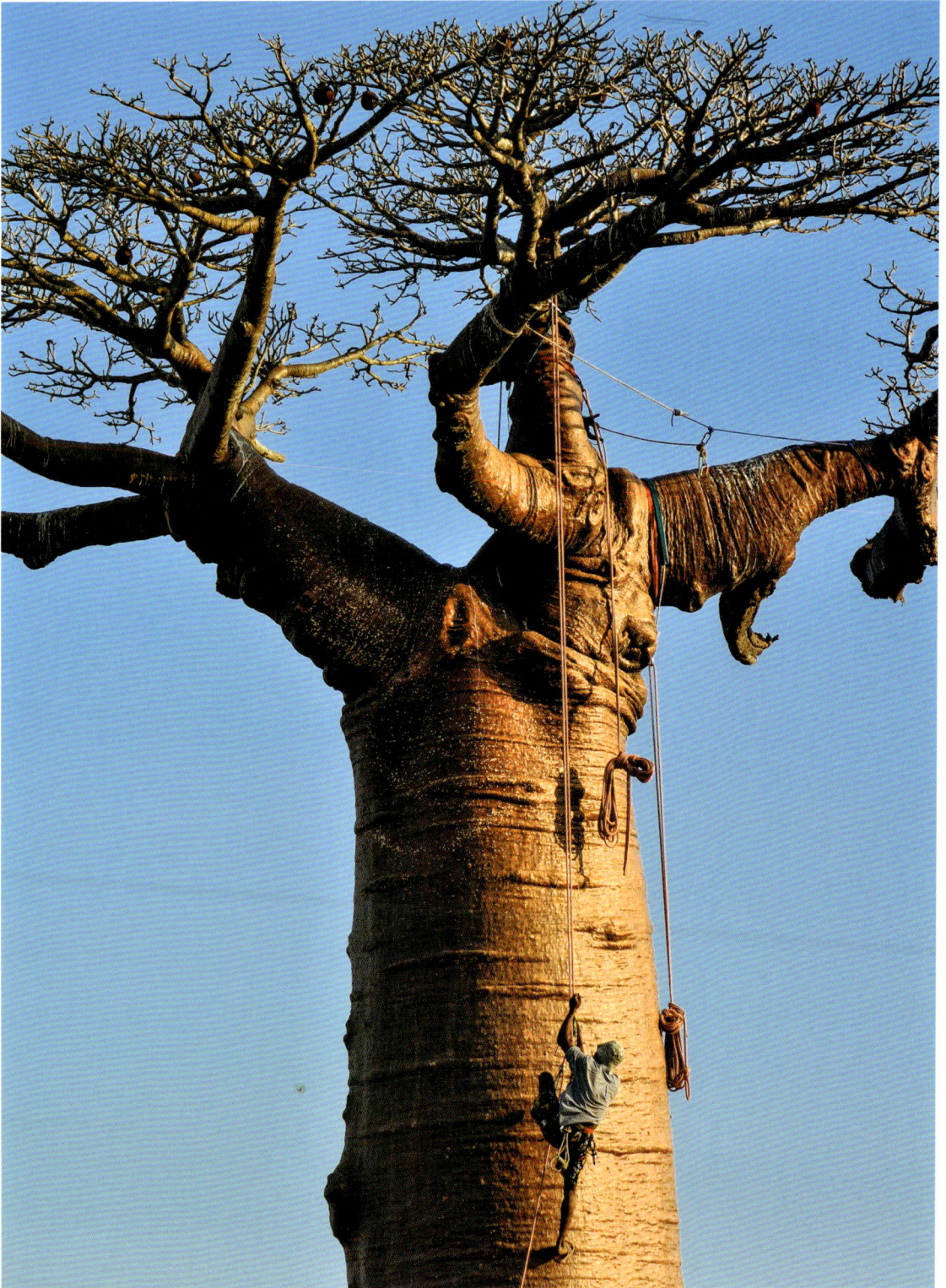

The following are examples of proverbs and literary quotations from around the world:

'Wisdom is like a baobab tree; no one individual can embrace it.'
Traditional, West Africa.

'If a sapling grows beneath a baobab, it will die a bush.'
Traditional, Central African Republic.

'It is at the foot of a baobab that one views a baobab best.'
Traditional, Senegal.

'Though he may sojourn long in the branches of the baobab, the partridge will never forget the nest of lowly brush where he was hatched.'
Ahmadou Kourouma (1927–2003) in *Waiting for the Wild Beasts to Vote.*

'Now there were some terrible seeds on the planet that was the home of the little prince; and these were the seeds of the baobab. The soil of that planet was infested with them. A baobab is something you will never, never be able to get rid of if you attend to it too late. It spreads over the entire planet. It bores clear through it with its roots. And if the planet is too small, and the baobabs are too many, they split it in pieces . . .'
Antoine de Saint-Exupéry, 1943, *The Little Prince.*

Opposite Visitors to the Avenue of Baobabs can watch the sunset from atop a baobab, or even sleep up in the canopy. Morondava. (L.J.)
Above Current and discontinued Malagasy banknotes. (A.P.)
Below A zebu carving in the bark of an *Adansonia grandidieri* at Tampolove, near Andavadoaka. Baobab wood and leaves are important resources for cattle in the spiny forest where food and water may be scarce during the long dry season. (L.J.)

Madagascar's baobabs

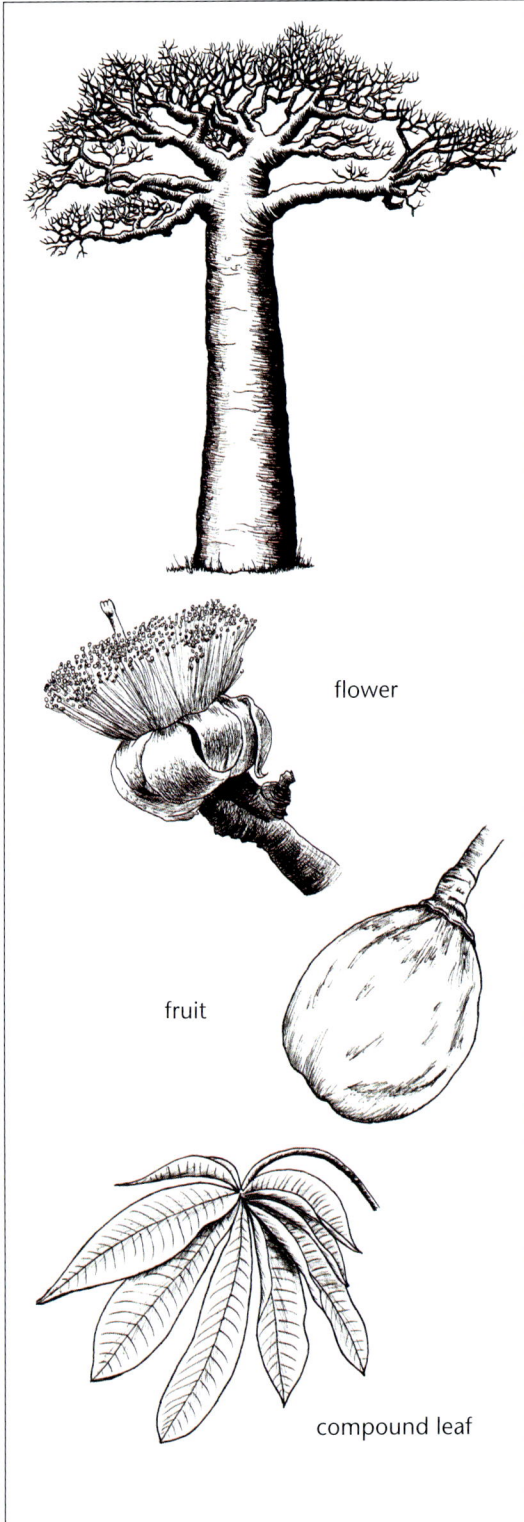

flower

fruit

compound leaf

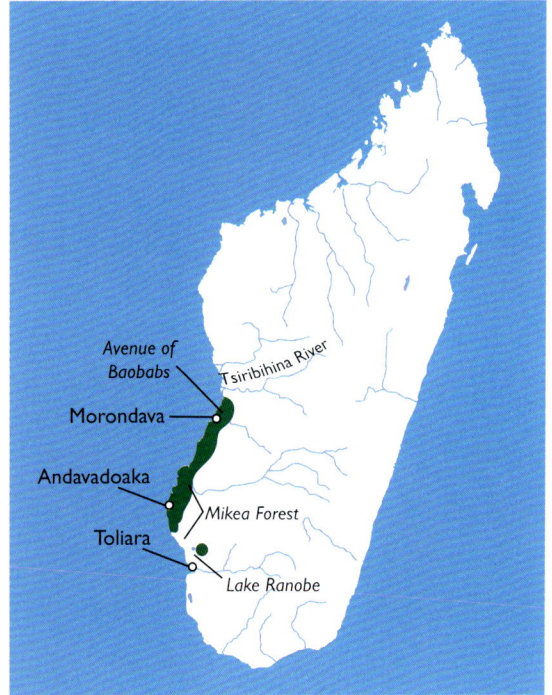

Avenue of Baobabs
Tsiribihina River
Morondava
Andavadoaka
Mikea Forest
Toliara
Lake Ranobe

Adansonia grandidieri
Baill., 1888

Common name Grandidier's Baobab (English),
Reniala, Renala (Malagasy)

Description The magnificent and statuesque
Adansonia grandidieri is one of the largest baobab
species in Madagascar and truly deserves its
Malagasy name *reniala*, meaning 'mother of
the forest'. Measuring 5–30m in height, it has a
cylindrical trunk typically reaching 3m in diameter,
though giant specimens with diameters of nearly
6m have been recorded near Morombe. The
species was described by the French botanist Henri
Baillon (1827–1895), who named it in honour
of the French geographer and naturalist Alfred
Grandidier (1836–1921).

The flat-topped crown holds aloft the palmate
leaves with 5–7 leaflets, which fall during the dry
season (April–October). The dark brown flower
buds produce erect white flowers from May to
August, while the tree is leafless. The fruits are
large and generally ovoid in shape with a relatively
thin shell (2.5–4mm thick), and are coated
with dense velvety brown hairs. They ripen in

November and December, and contain oil-rich, kidney-shaped seeds embedded within a soft matrix of fibres and powdery pulp. This pulp is rich in vitamin C and can be eaten raw or made into juice, while oil can be extracted from the seeds.

The Malagasy use the thick, fibrous bark to make rope, and sheets of the wood are used as roofing material; it is therefore common to see trunks of *A. grandidieri* scarred by repeated harvesting. Many people also harvest the leaves for cattle fodder during drought. In general, such practices pose little threat to the survival of this species; rather, it is the conversion of its forest habitat into agricultural land that is causing its decline. Indeed, in 1955 Henri Perrier de la Bâthie noted that 'this magnificent tree will soon be no more than a memory'. Fortunately, the situation was not quite as dire as that, but *A. grandidieri* is certainly in peril.

Distribution This species is native to the dry forests of western Madagascar, and its range stretches between the Tsiribihina River to the north and the limestone outcrops along the western edge of the Mikea Forest near Andavadoaka to the south. In the Morondava region, it forms the famous Avenue of Baobabs, which was recently declared a protected area. The site's local name, Ankorondrenala, literally means 'the place with the group of *renala*', though it became more widely known by its French name *Allée des baobabs* after the construction of the road connecting Morondava with Belo sur Tsiribihina.

Phenology Leaves present October–May, flowering occurs May–August, fruit ripens in November–December.

Conservation status Endangered.

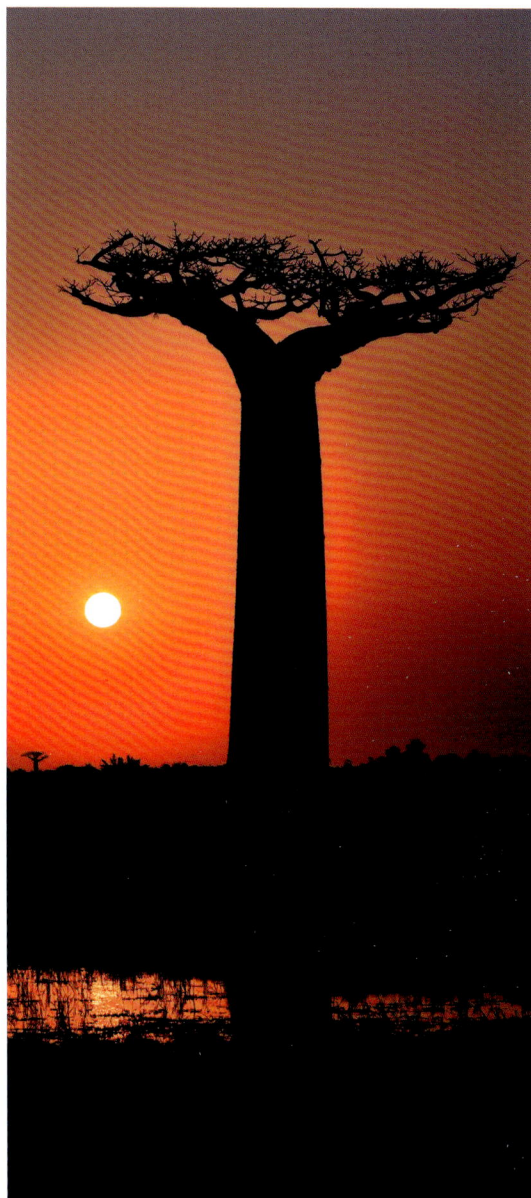

Previous spread Dawn over the baobab-rich forest of Kirindy-Mite, showing hundreds of *Adansonia grandidieri*. (V.V.)
Left A flower of *A. grandidieri*. (A.P.)
Above A majestic *A. grandidieri* at sunset near the Avenue of Baobabs. Morondava region. (L.J.)
Page 60 A dwarf *A. grandidieri* in spiny forest on limestone, with Andry Petignat's son providing scale. Near Andavadoaka. (A.P.)
Page 61 A typical, columnar specimen of *A. grandidieri* with bark-harvesting scars, in the transitional zone between the spiny forest and dry deciduous forest. Near Befandriana Sud. (A.P.)

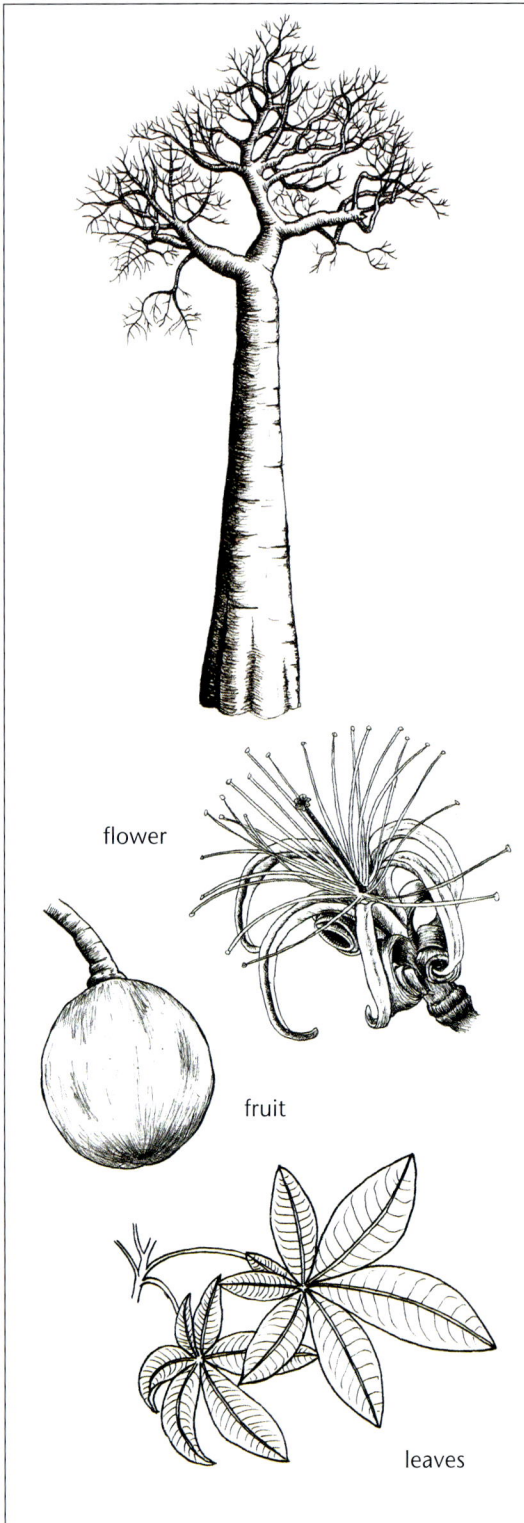

flower

fruit

leaves

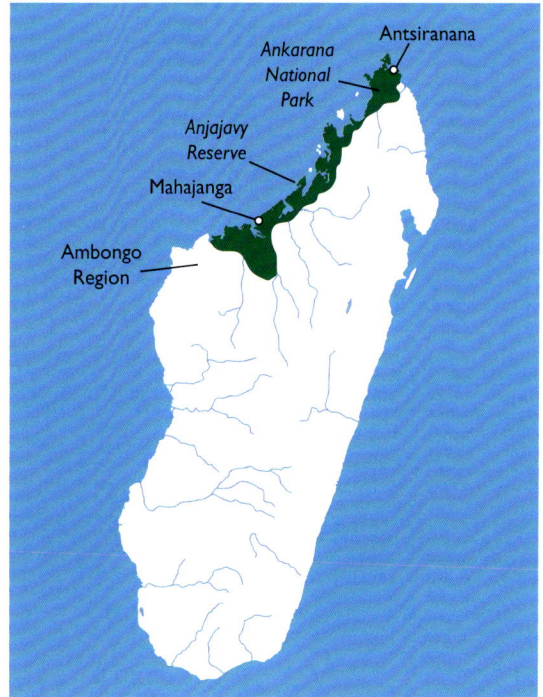

Adansonia madagascariensis
Baill., 1874

Synonym *Adansonia bernieri* Baill. ex Poiss., 1912
Common name Bozy, Bozy Malandy (Malagasy)
During his voyage to the island of Réunion,
Alphonse Charles Joseph Bernier (1802–1858),
a ship's doctor, visited the extreme north of
Madagascar and collected a large number of plant
specimens, including *Adansonia madagascariensis*.
It was the first Malagasy baobab species to be
officially described – by Baillon in 1874 – and
the now superfluous synonym *A. bernieri* was
dedicated to the early collector.
Description It is a massive tree, reaching 5–20m
in height, with a large, cylindrical or bottle-
shaped trunk up to 5m in diameter, with smooth,
pale grey bark. Its branches form an irregular
crown in the upper parts of the trunk. The leaves
are palmate, with 5–7 smooth leaflets attached
to a petiole of 60–70mm. The solitary flowers
are held erect or horizontal and have dark red
petals, making *A. madagascariensis* the only red-
flowered baobab, though occasionally yellow
flowers are also produced. The numerous pale

yellow-orange stamens are fused together at the base, and the style is pink or red. The velvety fruit is indehiscent, small (usually <10cm in length), spherical to oblong, with a woody pericarp 7–9mm thick. This species is very similar to *A. za*, but the fruits differ considerably in shape, and the flowers of *A. madagascariensis* tend to have petals shorter than the style, while those of *A. za* are considerably longer than the style.

Phenology Leaves present November–April, flowering occurs February–April, fruits ripen by November.

Distribution *Adansonia madagascariensis* is found in dry or moist deciduous forest in northern and northwestern Madagascar, from Antsiranana to the Ambongo region south of Mahajanga. It is amongst the dominant tree species in the dry deciduous forest of Ankarana National Park. It also grows along coastlines and off-shore islands in northern Madagascar, often alongside *A. suarezensis*.

Conservation status Near Threatened.

Top right *Adansonia madagascariensis* in full flower. Montagne des Français Protected Area. (L.J.)
Bottom right A flower of *A. madagascariensis*. (L.J.)
Below The velvety calyx of an *A. madagascariensis* flower. (A.P.)
Page 64 A stunted specimen of *A. madagascariensis* growing in coastal forest. Sakalava Bay, Antsiranana. (L.J.)
Page 65 A grove of *A. madagascariensis* growing by the sea on Cap Diego. (L.J.)

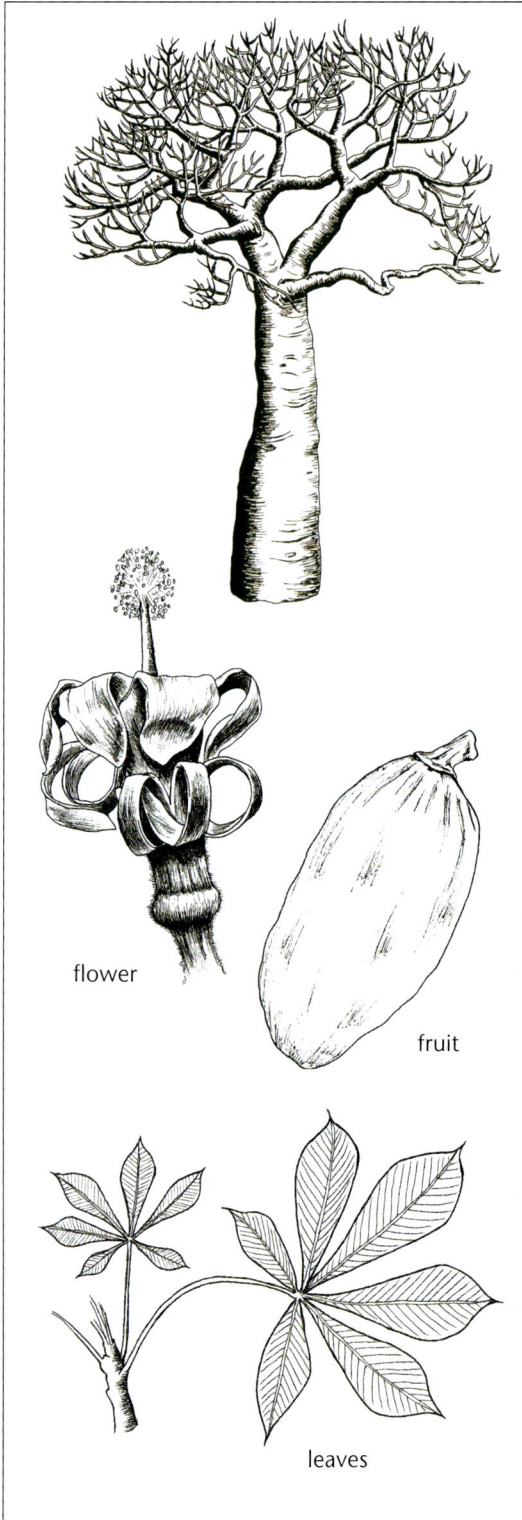

flower

fruit

leaves

Antsiranana

Montagne d'Ambre

Anivorano

Ankarana

Loky-Manambato

Ambilobe

Vohemar

Adansonia perrieri Capuron, 1960

Common name Bozy (Malagasy)

Adansonia perrieri, the most recently described Malagasy baobab, was long suspected to be a novel species but it wasn't confirmed until 1960 when René Capuron (1921–1971) was able to collect specimens from a flowering tree on the Ankarana Plateau. Capuron, who served as Principal Inspector for the Department of Water and Forest from 1948–1961 and collected nearly 4,000 herbarium specimens, named the species in honour of the French botanist Henri Perrier de la Bâthie.

Description *Adansonia perrieri* has a cylindrical or occasionally bottle-shaped trunk, reaching up to 30m in height and up to 3m in diameter, with smooth, pale grey bark. The palmate leaves have 5–11 leaflets, which are generally elliptic and pubescent (hairy). The elongated flower buds reveal pale yellow flowers at or just before leaf emergence. Flowers have cream-coloured petals that darken to yellow with age, a long white staminal tube topped with numerous pale yellow stamens, and a red style. The fruit is ovoid to oblong in shape, up to 25cm in length, and has a tough, fibrous pericarp 8–9mm thick and covered with short brown hairs.

Phenology Leaves present November–April, flowering occurs November–April, fruits ripen from October.

Distribution *Adansonia perrieri* is an extremely rare species that is restricted to a handful of sites in northern Madagascar, including the Ankarana and Montagne d'Ambre national parks, and Loky-Manambato Protected Area. It is found in evergreen rainforest and dry deciduous forest.

Conservation status Endangered.

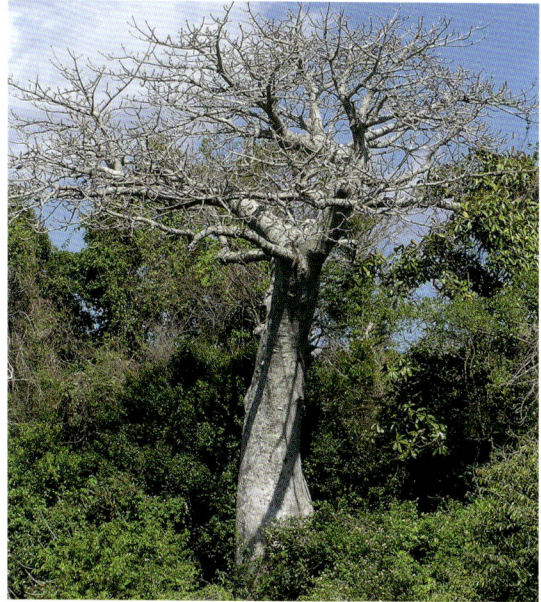

Left A flower of *Adansonia perrieri*. (D.B.)
Above *A. perrieri*, one of the rarest baobabs, growing near the road to Ankarana National Park. (C.Q.)
Below *A. perrieri* in riverine forest at Mahory Forest, near Ankarana National Park. (L.J.)

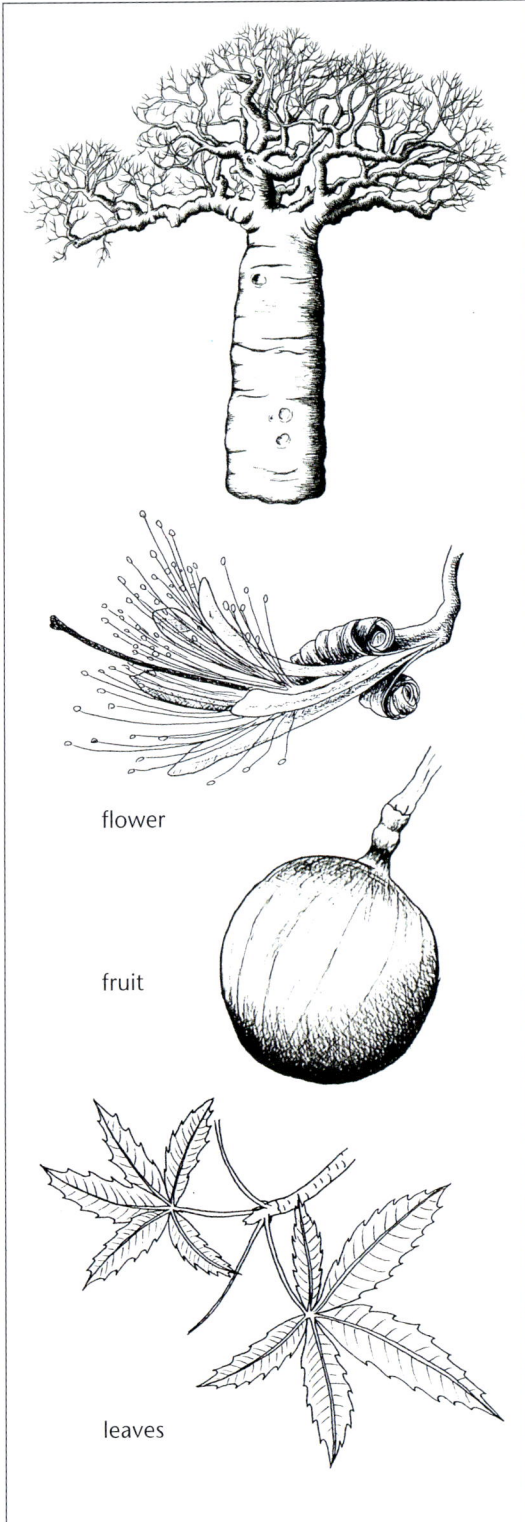

flower

fruit

leaves

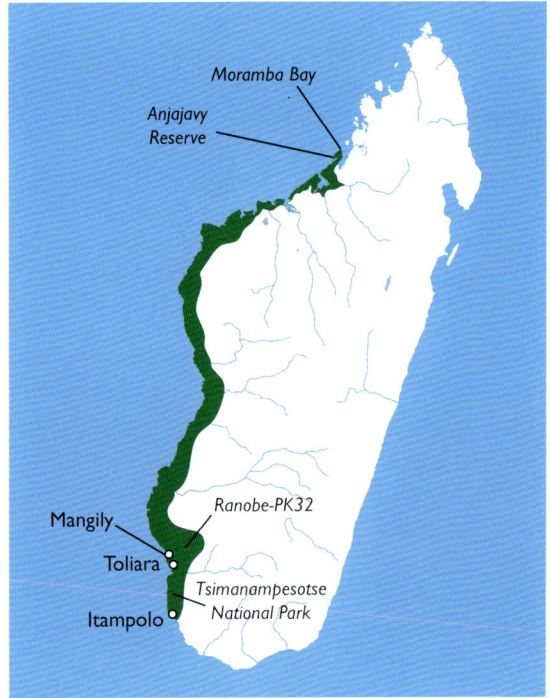

Adansonia rubrostipa
Jum. & H.Perrier, 1909

Synonym *Adansonia fony* Baill., 1890
Common name Fony, Bozy (Malagasy)
Description A small to medium tree reaching no more than 20m in height, *Adansonia rubrostipa* is considered to be the smallest of Madagascar's baobab species. The trunk is bottle-shaped, cylindrical, or occasionally tapering, usually with a distinct constriction just beneath the crown of branches. The bark is reddish-brown or copper-coloured, and tends to peel away in fine sheets revealing a thin photosynthetic layer beneath. The leaves are palmate, with 3–5 serrate (tooth-edged) leaflets, a characteristic that distinguishes it from all other baobab species. The flower bud is long and tubular, greenish-yellow on the outside, bright red within. The flowers emerge when the tree is in leaf, having bright yellow to orange-yellow petals, pale yellow stamens and a pink style. The fruits are roundish, with a hard shell 4–5mm thick that is coated with dense, orange-brown hairs.

The fruit pulp is used to make juice, and in Toliara whole fruits may be sold on the markets.

One tree may produce an average of 200kg of fruit, but the yield is very variable and some years no fruit is produced at all. The tree itself is very rarely used, but some people harvest the bark for making rope, and sheets of wood may be used for roofing.

Phenology Leaves present November–April, flowering occurs February–April, fruits ripen October–November.

Distribution This species extends along the west coast of Madagascar up to an altitude of 300m, from Moramba Bay in the north to Itampolo in the southwest. It grows in spiny forest and dry deciduous forest on well-drained red sand and calcareous soils, and on karstic limestone.

Conservation status Near Threatened.

Left The tall, columnar form of *Adansonia rubrostipa* at Anjajavy. (L.J.)

Above A typical bottle-shaped *A. rubrostipa* marks the 32-km point north of Toliara. Ranobe-PK32 Protected Area. (L.J.)

Below A flower of *A. rubrostipa*. (L.J.)

Page 70 A mature *A. rubrostipa* with ripening fruit. Andavadoaka. (L.J.)

Page 71 The wrinkled Grandmother Baobab in Tsimanampesotse National Park is at least 1,600 years old. (L.J.)

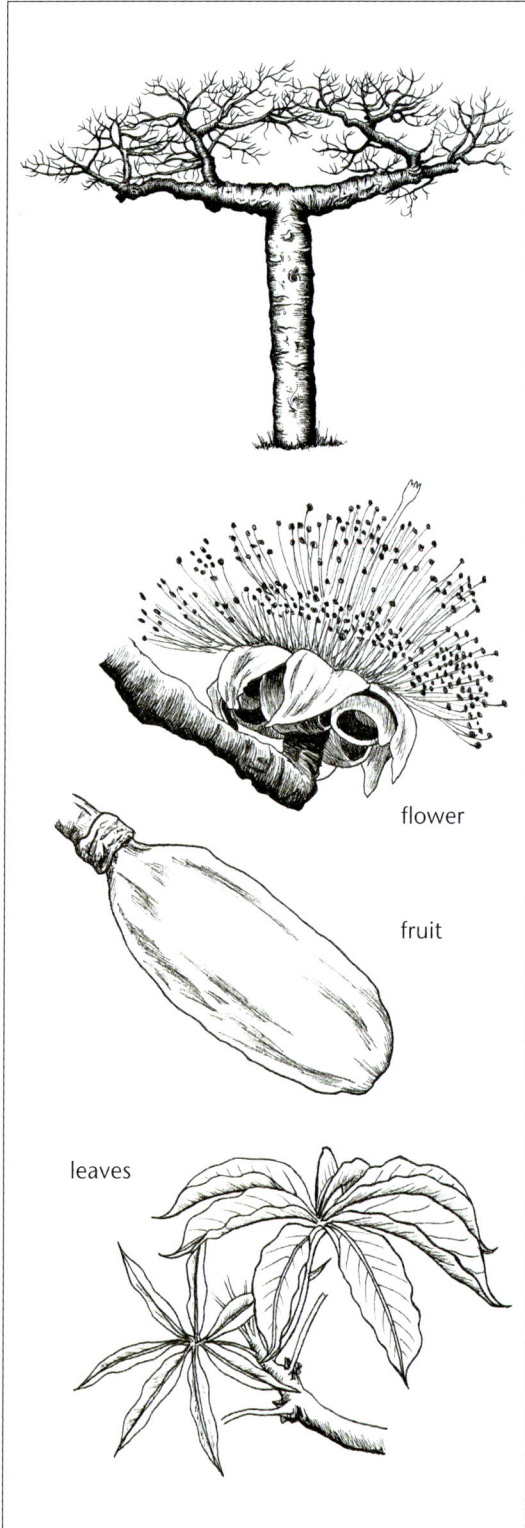

flower

fruit

leaves

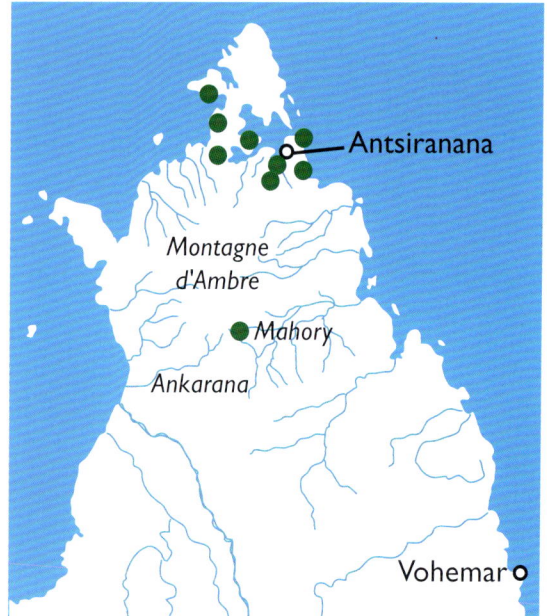

Antsiranana

Montagne
d'Ambre

Mahory

Ankarana

Vohemar

Adansonia suarezensis
H.Perrier, 1953

Common name Bozy, Bozy Mena, Tsitoloniny (Malagasy)

Description This baobab may reach up to 25m in height and 2m in diameter, with smooth grey to reddish-brown bark covering a thin green photosynthetic layer. The trunk may be cylindrical or tapering from bottom to top, and its large, horizontal branches are characteristic. The palmate leaves have 6–9 smooth leaflets, held upon a petiole 12–18cm long. The flower buds are erect and ovoid, the calyx greenish outside and creamy-white within. The flowers have white petals that turn yellow with age, a short staminal tube topped with 800–1,100 white filaments, and a white style. The fruits are large (20–40cm long and 8–14cm in diameter) and may weigh up to one kilogram. They are irregular in shape, from oblong-cylindrical to elongated ovoid; the pericarp is relatively thin (3–4mm) and fragile, containing few longitudinal fibres, and is covered with dense brown hairs. The seeds are the largest in the genus, reaching up to 20 x 15 x 14mm. The fruit and seeds are edible, while the bark is said to be a cure for diabetes and a substitute for quinine.

Phenology Leaves present December–April, flowering occurs from May–July, fruit ripens in November.

Distribution *Adansonia suarezensis* takes its scientific name from its region of origin, Diego Suarez (also known as Antsiranana). It grows in dry deciduous forest, especially on limestone. Shorter specimens can be seen close to the coast, e.g. along the road to Ramena and around the southern shores of Cap Diego, but taller trees may be found in less disturbed forest on the slopes of Montagne des Français and Windsor Castle. Although it was once believed to be entirely restricted to Antsiranana, a subpopulation has been found further south in the Mahory Forest.

Conservation status Endangered. This species is restricted to northern Madagascar, and its highly fragmented habitat is still disappearing due to wood extraction, grazing and shifting agriculture.

Top right A flower of *Adansonia suarezensis*. (D.B.)
Right The large seeds of *A. suarezensis*. (A.P.)
Below *A. suarezensis* growing in degraded forest, on the lower slopes of Montagne des Français, Antsiranana. (L.J.)
Overleaf A tall stand of *A. suarezensis* in Montagne des Français Protected Area, Antsiranana. (L.J.)

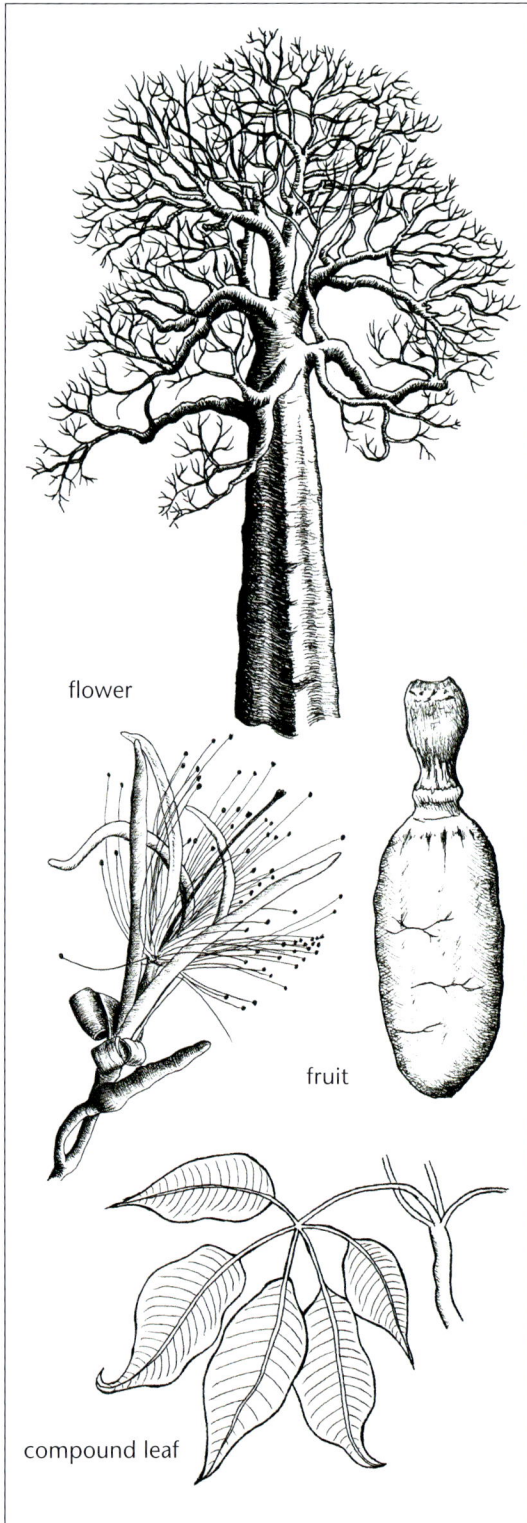

flower

fruit

compound leaf

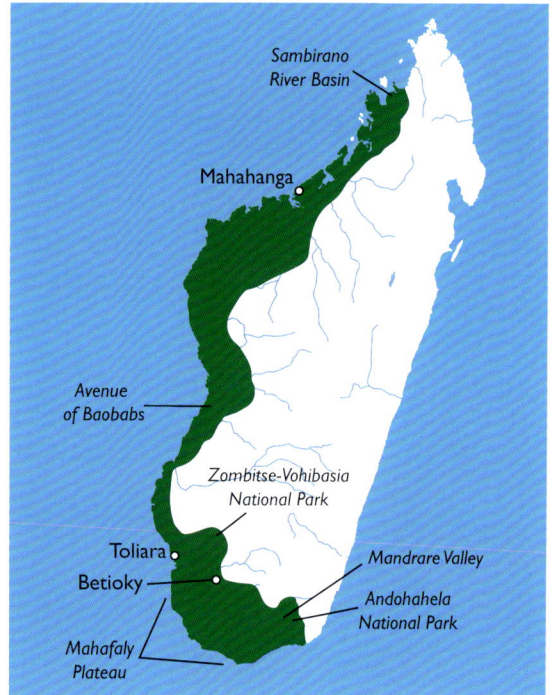

Sambirano
River Basin

Mahahanga

Avenue
of Baobabs

Zombitse-Vohibasia
National Park

Toliara

Betioky

Mandrare Valley

Andohahela
National Park

Mahafaly
Plateau

Adansonia za Baill., 1890

Synonym *Adansonia alba* Jum. & H.Perrier, 1910
Common name Za, Zaha, Bozy, Bozy Be,
Ringy (Malagasy)
Description *Adansonia za* is usually a tall tree,
reaching up to 30m in height and 3m in diameter.
The trunk is cylindrical or tapering, often with
irregular swellings. It is characterized by grey bark,
which is largely smooth, and a rounded crown
of ascending, tapering branches. The leaves are
palmate, with 5–8 smooth, elliptic-lanceolate leaflets
that are held on petiolules up to 3cm long. The
flower buds are erect to horizontal, elongated and
cylindrical, green outside and dark red within. The
flowers emerge simultaneously with or just after the
leaves, and have yellow petals, pale yellow stamens
and a dark red style. Fruits are 10–30cm long, often
ridged and variable in shape, from ovoid to oblong,
occasionally pointed, and have a distinctly swollen
peduncle. The pericarp is thick, tough and fibrous,
and is grey-black with a sparse covering of hairs.

The leaves and fruit are used locally to treat
diarrhoea, while the dry pulp mixed with Tamarind
(*Tamarindus indica*) fruit is used to treat dysentery.

Henri Perrier de la Bâthie recognized two varieties of this species, *A. za* var. *bozy* and *A. za* var. *boinensis*, which differ in the structure of their fruit and leaves. The former variety is endemic to the Sambirano River Basin of northwest Madagascar.

Phenology Leaves present in the rainy season October–April, flowering occurs November–February (earlier in the north), fruit ripens towards the end of the dry season.

Distribution This is the most widely distributed baobab species in Madagascar, and extends from the Andohahela National Park and the Mandrare River in southeastern Madagascar to the Boina region in the north. It is found in spiny forest, dry deciduous forest, subhumid forest (at Zombitse-Vohibasia National Park) and in savannah and scrubland up to 800m above sea level. In the northwest it is less common and tends to be concentrated along rivers.

Conservation status Near Threatened.

Top Long, grey fruits of *Adansonia za*. (A.P.)
Above Flower of *A. za*. (L.J.)
Top right Local people have carved a well into the trunk of this *A. za*. Between Betioky and Beheloka. (A.P.)
Bottom right Typical *A. za* trees in degraded spiny forest. Near Ambovombe. (A.P.)
Overleaf Majestic *A. za* stand in a sisal plantation in the Mandrare River valley, a popular *al fresco* dining spot for guests at the Mandrare River Camp. (L.J.)

Baobabs from elsewhere

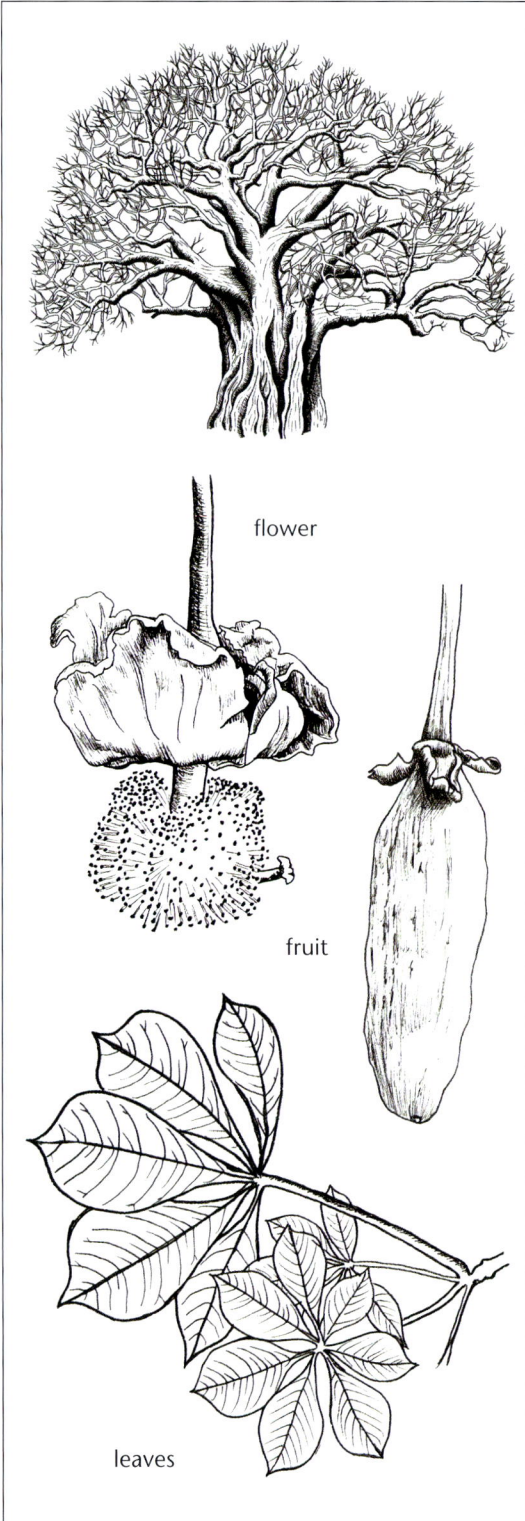

flower

fruit

leaves

Adansonia digitata L., 1759

Common name Hundreds of names have been recorded for this widespread species, including African Baobab, Dead Rat Tree, Cream of Tartar Tree, Mock Cotton Tree, Monkey-bread Tree, Upside-down Tree (English), Baobab D'afrique (French), Bozy Be, Boringy, Bontona, Reniala (Malagasy), Kremetert (Afrikaans), isiMuhu (Zulu), (Mbuyu (Swahili), Mowana (Tswana).

Description The African Baobab is without doubt the best known, most intensively studied and widely utilized of all baobab species. Its tangled branches are said to resemble roots, giving rise to the folktale that claims the tree draws its strength from the sky. All parts of the tree are used: the leaves are eaten as food and used medicinally to treat fevers. The fruit pulp is used as a fermenting agent in local brewing, as a substitute for cream of tartar in baking and to make a juice rich in vitamin C. The seeds can be eaten fresh, or roasted, fermented, ground or dried for use in sauces or as a coffee substitute. The roots yield a red dye, and the bark is used locally to treat fevers and poisoning. Hollow trunks have been put to a wide range of uses, including bars, storage barns and even toilets! One well-known African Baobab is found in the centre of Mahajanga in western Madagascar, where it lies at the centre of a roundabout. The largest known specimen is the two-stemmed Sunland Baobab, near Modjadjiskloof; it measures 47m in circumference and has been transformed by its owners into a bar and wine cellar that can hold up to 50 people.

This iconic species is characterized by an elephantine trunk with grey bark and an enormous, irregular crown. The trunk may reach up to 30m in height and more than 10m in diameter. Trees with multiple, buttressed stems are common, and old specimens are often hollow. The leaves are palmate, with 5–7 smooth leaflets, which vary greatly in size. Flower buds are roughly spherical, greenish on the outside and creamy within, and, unlike those of other baobabs, they are borne on a long, pendulous stalk 15–90cm long. The flowers have white, somewhat crumpled petals, white stamens and a white style that is usually bent at a right angle. The fruits are variable in shape, from round to ovoid or oblong-cylindrical, with a woody pericarp 8–10mm thick and covered in velvety yellow-brown or greenish hairs.

Phenology Varies from region to region. Leaves fall in the dry season; flowering may occur in the presence or absence of leaves during the dry or wet season.

Distribution *A. digitata* is native to sub-Saharan Africa, where it occurs naturally in around 30 countries. However, this culturally and economically important baobab has been widely introduced to tropical and subtropical countries around the world, including Madagascar and the Mascarene Islands, India, Sri Lanka, China, Hawaii, Florida and Barbados. It was probably introduced to Madagascar hundreds of years ago by Arab traders.

Conservation status Least Concern.

Previous spread A stunted *Adansonia digitata* on Khubu Island, Makgadikgadi Pans National Park, Botswana. (S.V.)
Bottom The famous *A. digitata* growing at the centre of a roundabout in Mahajanga, Madagascar. (B.R.)
Inset Flowers of *A. digitata*. (L.J.)
Overleaf A large *A. digitata* in the Kruger National Park. (L.J.)

flower

fruit

leaves

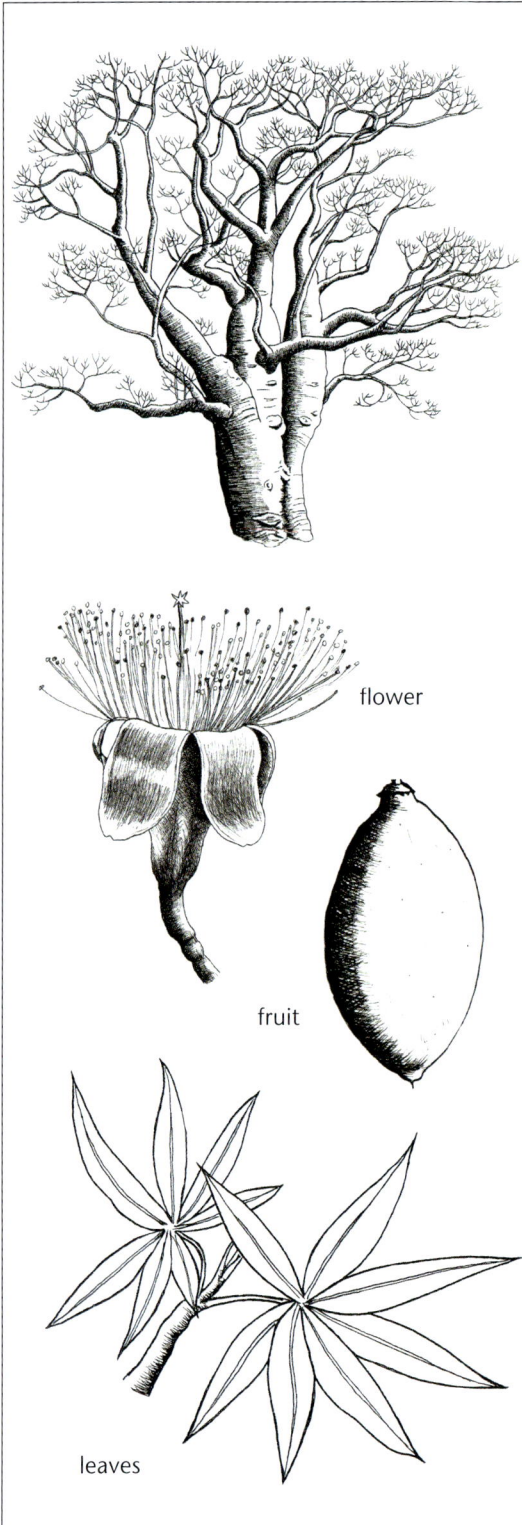

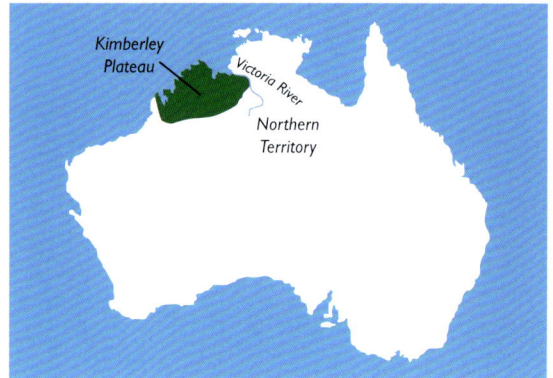

Adansonia gregorii F.Muell., 1857

Synonym *Adansonia gibbosa* (A.Cunn.) Guymer ex D.A.Baum, 1995
Common name Boab, Dead Rat Tree, Gouty Stem Tree (English), Kuruwan, Jamulang, Gadawori (Aboriginal Australian)

At the beginning of the 18th century, the British botanist Allan Cunningham (1791–1839) recorded the Australian baobab, taking it for a member of the genus *Capparis* and thus named it *C. gibbosa*. However, it was the German botanist Ferdinand von Müller (1825–1896) who formally recognized its taxonomic affinities with the African Baobab.

The fruits vaguely resemble dead rats hanging from the branches, giving the Boab its other common name, the Dead Rat Tree. Despite this grisly name, the fruits are eaten, as they are rich in vitamin C. The trees themselves have also been used as emergency water stores, the bark is employed in rope-making, and the leaves and gum exuded from damaged wood can be eaten.

A large hollow Boab growing south of Derby is said to have been used as a temporary jail for Aboriginal prisoners on the last stage of their journey to the courthouse in the 1890s, and was able to hold up to a dozen people. However, there is no written evidence to verify this story. The tree still stands today; it is indeed vast and nearly spherical; its ceiling is 6m high and, apart from the entrance door, there are two other holes that may have provided the prisoners with ventilation. Today this tree is a popular tourist attraction.

Description It is a small tree of rarely more than 10m in height, often with multiple trunks and a marked constriction in girth beneath the branches giving it the shape of a bottle. The bark is smooth, grey to greyish-orange. The leaves are palmate with 5–9 leaflets, smooth to slightly hairy. The buds are erect to horizontal, pale green outside and creamy-white within. Flowers emerge just before or just after the leaves, with cream to white petals, white to pale yellow stamens, and a white style. The fruit is spherical to ovoid, with a brittle pericarp 3–4mm thick (often cracking while still on the tree), which is covered in green or brown hairs.

Phenology Leaves present November–March, flowering occurs November–January, fruits ripen May–December.

Distribution *A. gregorii* is the only baobab species native to Australia, and it is limited to the Kimberley region and the Victoria River area of northwest Northern Territory. It is found in wooded grasslands near rocky ranges, along seasonal streams and on the floodplains of large rivers, especially in open areas subject to frequent fires.

Conservation status Not yet evaluated.

Below The fruit of *Adansonia gregorii* has the most fragile shell of all the baobab species. (B.F.)
Top right *A. gregorii* in burned pastureland. (B.F.)
Bottom right A flower of *A. gregorii*. (B.F.)
Overleaf These *A. gregorii* are thriving in grassland subject to frequent fires. (S.N.)

Look-alike species

In Madagascar, baobabs are often confused with other succulent, bottle-shaped trees such as *Moringa drouhardii*, *Delonix floribunda* and *Pachypodium geayi*. Although superficially similar, these species are not closely related to baobabs. They have come to resemble each other through a process called convergent evolution, whereby unrelated species living in similar conditions develop the same adaptations and appearance. In southern and western Madagascar, the climate is hot and dry, and the rainy season is short and often unpredictable. Succulent, swollen stems and branches, pale, peeling bark and deciduous leaves are all adaptations to a harsh, unforgiving climate.

On the following pages, we will present the species most commonly confused with baobabs, and help you to identify them.

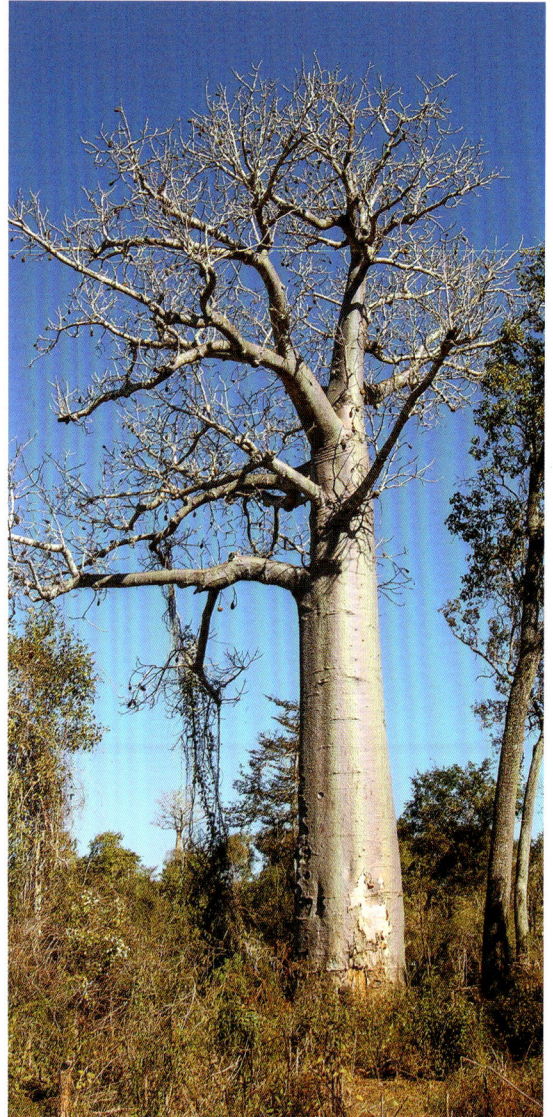

Above With their swollen trunks and silver-grey bark, *Delonix floribunda* (left) and *Adansonia za* (right) can look very similar, but are in fact unrelated. These two tree species occur in the hot, dry climate of southern Madagascar's spiny forests, and have developed similar characteristics through convergent evolution. (L.J.)

Delonix spp. (Fabaceae)

Common name Flame Tree (English), Flamboyant (French), Malamasafoy, Fengoky (Malagasy)

Description There are nine species of *Delonix* in Madagascar, all of which are endemic. Most species have swollen, cigar- or bottle-shaped trunks, and several have reddish-brown to grey bark that peels off in sheets. However, they rarely grow to the same massive height and girth as *Adansonia*. Like baobabs, *Delonix* have large, showy flowers, but they are smaller and differ greatly in structure. The leaves are composite, bipinnate with many small leaflets, and *Delonix* fruits are long, narrow, woody pods.

Previous spread On the Mahafaly Plateau in southwestern Madagascar, gold-coloured *Adansonia rubrostipa* grow alongside white *Pachypodium geayi*, which are sometimes mistakenly referred to as baobabs. (V.V.)

Right Papery, peeling bark is a distinctive feature of many *Delonix* species. (L.J.)

Below *D. floribunda* growing on the limestone plateau at Tsimanampesotse National Park. (L.J.)

Inset bottom left *D. decaryi* flowers. (L.J.)

Inset bottom right The fruits of all *Delonix* species are long, flat, woody pods. (L.J.)

Givotia madagascariensis
(Euphorbiaceae)

Common name Farafatsy, Farafatse (Malagasy)

Description *Givotia madagascariensis* is characterized by a swollen, cylindrical trunk with smooth, grey bark. It grows in dry deciduous and spiny forest in western and southwestern Madagascar. *Givotia* wood is soft, light and strong, and is much sought after by Vezo fisherman for making a *lakana*, the traditional outrigger canoe. It is most likely to be confused with *Adansonia za* because of the similar coloration and shape. However, unlike *Adansonia* species, *Givotia* has simple, lobed leaves, and it has compound inflorescences with small, whitish-yellow flowers.

Below The bark is generally smooth and shiny, though it may become creased or pitted in mature trees. (L.J.)

Top right *Givotia madagascariensis* trunks are often contorted or crooked, with creases in the bark appearing at bends. (L.J.)

Bottom right The flowers of *G. madagascariensis* are small and easily overlooked. (L.J.)

Moringa drouhardii (Moringaceae)

Common name Flour-sack Tree (English), Maroserana (Malagasy)

Description *Moringa drouhardii* has distinctive grey-white bark and a swollen trunk, which may reach up to 2m in diameter. Its wood is water-rich and fibrous, closely resembling baobab wood. It has short, twisting branches that often form a dense, rounded crown. However, the leaves, flowers and fruit are all easily distinguishable from those of the baobabs. *M. drouhardii* has compound leaves, bipinnate with numerous small leaflets. The inflorescences contain many small, yellow flowers that attract clouds of insects, while the fruits are long, green pods containing whitish pyramid-shaped seeds 2–3cm long.

Below A ripe fruit of *Moringa drouhardii*. (L.J.)
Top right *M. drouhardii* inflorescences are panicles made up of small yellow flowers. (L.J.)
Bottom right *M. drouhardii* growing on limestone. Sarodrano, near Toliara. (A.P.)

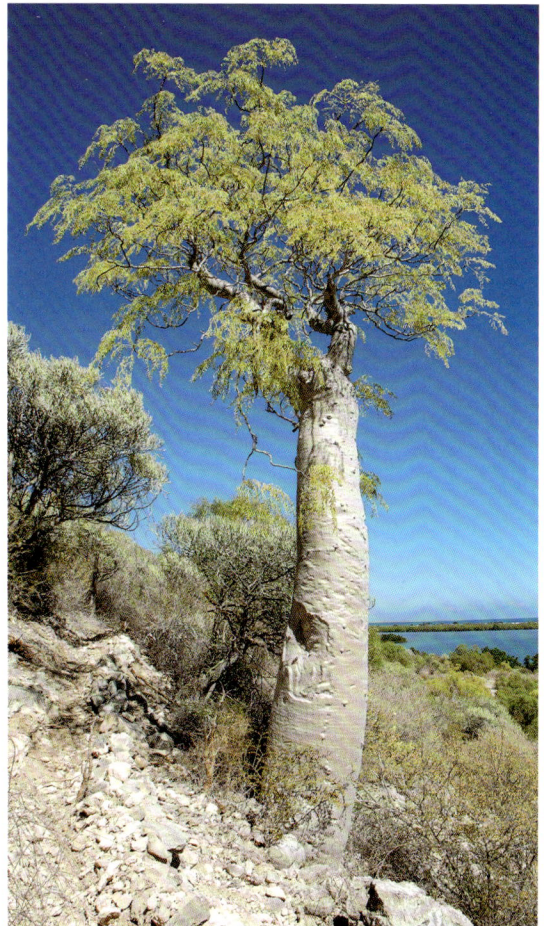

Pachypodium spp. (Apocynaceae)

Common name Elephant-foot Tree (English), Vontake (Malagasy)

Description The genus *Pachypodium* contains around 25 species, 20 of which are endemic to Madagascar. They are variable in form, from dwarf species a few centimetres high to cigar- or bottle-shaped trees up to 5m tall, with spiny trunks and/or branches. In contrast with *Adansonia*, the trunk and branches are usually spiny and the leaves of bottle-shaped species of *Pachypodium* are simple and elongated, growing from the stem in whorls. The widespread *P. geayi* and *P. lameri* have grey-white bark and white, windmill-shaped flowers. *P. rosulatum* var. *gracilius*, which grows on the Isalo Massif, is often incorrectly referred to as a dwarf baobab.

Below *Pachypodium rosulatum* var. *gracilius*. Isalo. (L.J.)
Top right *P. geayi* has a bottle-shaped trunk with grey-white bark. Tsimanampesotse National Park. (L.J.)
Bottom right Rows of worn spines spiral up the trunk of this mature *P. geayi*. Arboretum d'Antsokay, Toliara. (L.J.)
Inset bottom right Flowers of *P. mikea*. PK32-Ranobe. (L.J.)

Above Intricate spiral patterns cover the trunk of this *Adansonia grandidieri*. The cause of these markings remains unknown, though some believe them to be the result of a fungus. Andavadoaka. (L.J.)

Overleaf A giant *A. grandidieri* towers over a small Sakalava village. Near Morondava. (V.V.)

Pages 100–101 A collage of baobab trees, bark, leaves, flowers and fruit. **Left to right, top row:** *A. rubrostipa* flowers, *A. suarezensis*, *A. suarezensis* bark, *A. rubrostipa* fruit, *A. grandidieri*, *A. grandidieri* fruit. **Second row:** Atypical *A. za* fruit, *A. rubrostipa* seedling, *A. grandidieri* stamens, *A. madagascariensis* leaves, *A. madagascariensis* stigma, *A. madagascariensis* flower. **Third row:** *A. madagascariensis* flower, hollow *A. grandidieri*, *A. digitata* flower, *A. rubrostipa* flower, *A. grandidieri*, *A. rubrostipa* and Standing's Day Gecko. **Fourth row:** *A. suarezensis*, *A. grandidieri* bark, typical *A. za* fruit, *A. madagascariensis* flower bud, *A. rubrostipa* fruit, and *A. grandidieri* flower. (L.J. and A.P.)

Pages 102–103 A stunted *A. rubrostipa* under the wheeling stars at Tsimanampesotse National Park. (L.J.)

GLOSSARY

Angiosperm: Any of a class (Angiospermae) or division (Magnoliophyta) of vascular plants that have the ovules and seeds enclosed in an ovary, form the embryo and endosperm by double fertilization, and typically have each flower surrounded by a perianth composed of two sets of floral envelopes comprising the calyx and corolla – also called a flowering plant.

Calyx: The outermost envelope of a flower, comprising a number of sepals.

Compound: Describes a leaf that is divided into two or more parts (known as leaflets) attached to a single petiole.

Cuticle: A thin, non-cellular layer covering the outer surface of plant stems and leaves, which helps to prevent water loss.

Deciduous: Describes a tree or shrub that sheds its leaves during unfavourable seasons, or a forest composed of deciduous trees.

Endemic: A species of organism that is confined to a particular geographical region.

Family: In taxonomic classification, a category of related organisms comprising one or more genera. Scientific names of plant families usually end in –ceae.

Genus (plural genera): In taxonomic classification, a category of related organisms comprising one or more species.

Glabrous: Smooth, lacking hairs or bristles.

Herbaceous: Describes plants that are non-woody and wither after each growing season.

Hermaphrodite: A plant or animal that has both male and female reproductive organs.

Indehiscent: Describes a fruit that does not open when ripe to release the seeds.

Lanceolate: Tapering to a point like the head of a lance.

Leaflet: A division of a compound leaf.

Oblong: Having a shape that is longer than it is wide, with a roughly rectangular form.

Palmate: Describes leaves that have five or more lobes arising from a single point, spreading like fingers from a hand.

Pericarp: The part of a fruit that surrounds the seeds.

Petiole: The leaf stalk.

Petiolule: The stalk of a leaflet, joining the leaflet to the leaf stalk.

Phylogeny: The evolutionary history of a species, genus or group.

Pubescent: Having hairs or bristles.

Species: A subdivision of a genus considered to be the basic biological classification, containing individuals that resemble each other and that may interbreed.

Stamen: The male reproductive organ of a flower, consisting of a stalk or filament bearing a pollen-producing anther.

Stoma (plural stomata): A tiny pore in the outer layer of a leaf or stem through which gaseous exchange takes place.

Succulent: A plant that has thick, fleshy, water-storing leaves, stems or roots.

Tegument: The outer covering of a seed.

Variety: In botanical terms, a taxonomic category of related organisms of a rank below species. Varieties may arise naturally or by selective plant breeding.

Zoochory: The dispersal of plant fruits and seeds by animals.

Opposite The Four-windowed Baobab (*A. grandidieri*) is completely hollow, its cool interior giving shelter to travellers on hot days. Belitsake, near Morombe. (L.J.)

BIBLIOGRAPHY

Baum, D.A. 1995. The comparative pollination and floral biology of baobabs (*Adansonia-Bombacaceae*). *Annals of the Missouri Botanical Garden* 82: 322–348.

Baum, D.A. 1995. A systematic revision of *Adansonia* (Bombacaceae). *Annals of the Missouri Botanical Garden* 82: 440–470.

Baum, D.A. 2003. Bombacaceae, *Adansonia*. Baobab, Bozy, Fony, Renala, Ringy, Za. In *The Natural History of Madagascar*, eds S.M. Goodman and J.P. Benstead, pp. 339–342. Chicago: The University of Chicago Press.

Baum, D.A., Small, R.L. and Wendel, J.F. 1998. Biogeography and floral evolution of baobabs (*Adansonia*, Bombacaceae) as inferred from multiple data sets. *Systematic Biology* 47: 181–207.

Cabanis, Y., Chabouis, L. and Chabouis, F. 1969. *Végétaux et Groupements Végétaux de Madagascar et des Mascareignes*, Vols 1, 2 and 3. Tananarive: Bureau pour le Développement de la Production Agricole.

Chapotin, S.M., Razanameharizaka, J.H. and Holbrook, N.M. 2005. Baobab tree (*Adansonia*) in Madagascar use stored water to flush new leaves but not to support stomatal opening before the rainy season. *New Phytologist* 169: 549–559.

Chapotin, S.M., Razanameharizaka, J.H. and Holbrook, N.M. 2006. Water relations of baobab trees (*Adansonia* spp. L.) during the rainy season: does stem water buffer daily water deficits? *Plant, Cell and Environment* 29: 1,021–1,032.

Goodman, S.M. and Benstead, J.P. (eds) 2003. *The Natural History of Madagascar*. Chicago: University of Chicago Press.

IUCN. 2011. *IUCN Red List of Threatened Species*. Version 2014. 2. www.iucnredlist.org.

Pakenham, T. 2004. *The Remarkable Baobab*. London: W.W. Norton & Company.

Patrut, A., von Reden, K.F., Danthu, P., Leong Pock-Tsy, J-M., Patrut, R.T. and Lowy, D.A. Searching for the oldest baobab of Madagascar: radiocarbon investigation of large *Adansonia rubrostipa* trees. *Plos One* DOI10:1371.

Patrut, A., von Reden, K.F., Mayne, D.H., Lowy, D.A. and Patrut, R.T. 2013. AMS radiocarbon investigation of the African baobab: searching for the oldest tree. *Nuclear Instruments and Methods in Physics Research B* 294: 622–626.

Perrier de la Bâthie, H. 1955. Bombacacées. In *Flore de Madagascar et des Comores*, ed. H. Humbert, pp. 1–17. Paris: Botanical Society of France.

Petignat, A. and Cooke, B. 2009. *Guide des Plantes Succulentes du Sud-Ouest de Madagascar*. Toliara: Arboretum d'Antsokay and Phyto-Logic.

Rauh, W. 1998. *Succulent and Xerophytic Plants of Madagascar*, Vols I and 2. Mill Valley, USA: Strawberry Press.

Razanameharizaka, J., Grouzis, M., Ravelomanana, D. and Danthu, P. 2006. Seed storage behaviour and seed germination in African and Malagasy baobabs (*Adansonia* species). *Seed Science Research* 16: 83–88.

Schatz, G.E. 2001. *Generic Tree Flora of Madagascar*. Kew: Missouri Botanical Garden and Royal Botanic Garden.

Wickens, G.E. and Lowe, P. 2008. *The Baobabs: Pachycauls of Africa, Madagascar and Australia*. London: Springer.

Opposite Baobabs provide important resources for wildlife. They give food and shelter for dozens of species of invertebrate, nesting sites for birds, and can house reptiles such as this rare Banded Day Gecko (*Phelsuma standingi*). (L.J.)

Overleaf A group of columnar *Adansonia grandidieri* produce a spectacular landscape. Avenue of Baobabs, near Morondava. (L.J.)

INDEX

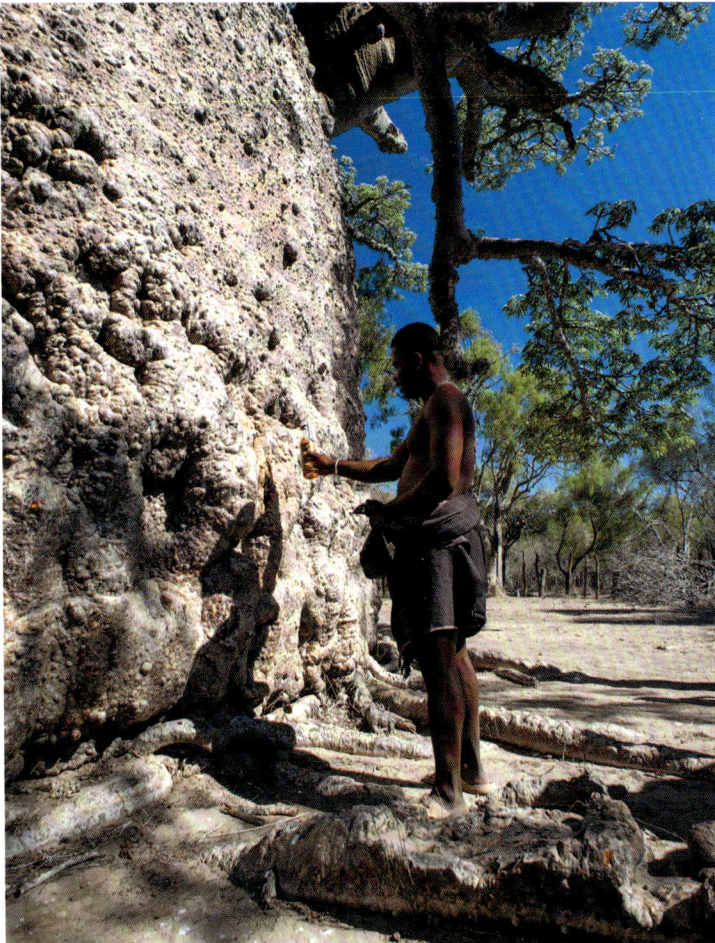

Above Visitors to the sacred Tsitakakoiky Baobab at Andombiry must bring offerings of rum and tobacco. These gifts are used in a traditional rite performed at the base of the great tree. (L.J.)